College on a Dime

2nd Edition

Lorenzo Ruccetti

For all the late night project teams, last minute study groups, hardcore STAT gurus, weekend warriors, band mates, co-workers, co-pilots and co-conspirators who burn the candle from both ends. The world is yours.

For Lena.

For you.

CONTENTS

Welcome to the future!

Freedom! Your first car! No curfews! And pizza! So much pizza!

College is all this and more. While it is a time of self-exploration, limitless possibilities and little responsibility, it is also late night cramming, group projects and rummaging under the couch for a) pizza or b) pizza money. If you're lucky, you'll find c) both.

This guide is designed to be a useful tool in maximizing the opportunities afforded to you with a college education, without burdening you with soul-crushing college debt. College time is an awesome time to be alive, but if it leaves you with more debt than you can pay, you may find yourself with both a forgettable Spring Break in Miami and an unforgettable credit card bill. Coming from personal experience, that debt lingers longer than the champagne! And the hangover!

While all of the information in this book is useful (full disclosure: I am the author and I am biased) it can be used as a DVD; simply go to the right chapter to get the information you need, when you need it.

Above all, best of luck to you in college and your future!

1 BEFORE COLLEGE

How much is your pride worth to you?

The question is simple, but the answer is difficult. And answering it honestly is even more difficult. Can you put a monetary value on your pride? Tough question.

Going to college on a dime requires a complete paradigm shift in the way you think and act. It is not for the faint of heart. Getting a diploma without getting into lots of debt requires a lot of courage, humility, perseverance and inner strength. So if you're okay with lacking these traits, feel free to put the book down and go back to more fun activities, like playing video games. You might find yourself five years from now regretting that you wasted your free time blowing away storm troopers when you could have found a way that would have enabled you to begin your adult life with a clean financial slate. The choice is yours.

You'll be making many choices like this in your lifetime. These decisions are a reflection of who you are, where you come from, and where you're going. They say more about you than you know. They say what your priorities are. So, can you place a monetary value on your pride?

In fact, you do it every day. It is in the choices you make - choices great and small. It ends with big choices, like what car or house you choose, but it starts with the little choices, like what to eat at a restaurant. Quickly it becomes choices between this pair of shoes you simply must have, and that pair of shoes you simply must have. The answer is "choose both," right?

Perhaps the correct answer is to buy neither (yes, neither - I told you, complete paradigm shift). Many of the choices you make with your money as a junior in high school will influence the choices you make as a junior in college. Your "spending style" is formed when you are first given respectable amounts of money and have the ability to spend it. Usually that begins when you are 16 and suddenly find yourself with a little bit of money in your wallet or purse setting next to the keys to the family wagon. Now you can race off to the mall to check out what's in for the fall. After all, you need to - it's a priority. Right?

High school is a great time to start learning how to budget your money (and time). It certainly beats learning this valuable lesson the hard way when you're halfway through your first semester at State and you have no money, no food, and a late term paper. I've watched as fellow students pawned laptops, guitars, bikes – even a car – to get some food money or pay for lab fees. It didn't have to happen to them, and it doesn't have to happen to you.

I'm not going to tell you that a one size fits all budget is exactly what you need. In fact, there is no single way to budget your money. Some of you should adopt a budget that works for you. Some of you might consider adapting yourself to a working budget. You know yourself better than any financial analyst, and if you're completely honest with yourself, you'll be able to decide what works best for you. While I will not tell you exactly what you should do with your money, I will tell you my secret that has worked extremely well, and which anyone can follow. But it's a big secret.

Don't tell anyone. My miracle method to budgeting money and staying out of debt in college is this highly complex formula of numbers and principles that would make Harvard's business professors blush. Quiet. Is no one watching? Okay, here goes:

Live on less money than you make.

That's right! Step up and witness the amazing new wonder budget! You'll find money you never knew you had! You'll find money here. You'll find money there. You'll find money coming out of your.....ears. I employed this method of budgeting when I was 18, and the results were incredible! This secret budgeting tonic comes from an old family recipe handed down to me from my grandfather, who learned of this miracle cure during the Great Depression. Guaranteed to work wonders or your money back!

A rather simple formula. Live on less money than you make. I know it seems like a foreign concept, especially today, where everything is obtained instantly on credit and a person's worth is determined by their beacon score. But remember: paradigm shift. If you live on less money than you make, then at the end of the day you will have more money to live on. Instead of dreading the credit card bill, you will find a bank account with actual money in it! What a concept! This simple way of budgeting your money will always leave you with more money and less debt. I promise you that many of our parents are just now understanding and adopting this way of thinking. If only they knew what you now know.

So what are you going to do with this secret? Will you practice it and reap the many benefits? Will you discuss how it works in theory but not in reality? Will you simply file it into the back of your brain as you read on? Will you give up and do battle with those storm troopers? The choice is yours. What kind of choice will you make? What will be your priority?

Something you should determine before you leave high school is how much money you have right now to pay for college. What kind of shape is your bank account in? Do you even have a bank account? How much money you have right now should give you a starting point to begin saving up funds for college. Also, a look at your current funds will help you determine which school you choose to attend. If you only have $27 in a change jar, then maybe even with your genius brain you might be better off starting at a local community college than at MIT. Of course, the question is begged, if your financial situation consists of a change jar with net assets of $27, are you really a genius?

Your cynical self might proclaim that you've got parents, grandparents, long lost cousins and tonight's winning lottery tickets to cover what your bank account does not. And while for many, this is true, we cannot count on that until it is in your hands.

As an example, I had a good friend in high school (let's call him Johnny) who managed to save $3,700 his senior year working odd jobs. Three months before graduation Johnny's parents bought a house, using $3,000 of his savings, along with other money to get the monthly mortgage payments into a manageable amount. It was their full intent to pay back the $3,000 before tuition became due in August, but unfortunately for Johnny, it never materialized. Eventually his parents paid him back, but it was too late to help with college expenses, and Johnny had to change the college he went to, and thus, much of his career trajectory. I tell you this story to illustrate that sometimes a sure thing is not as sure as we think.

How much time do you have before you graduate? Are you a sophomore who is just now old enough to work a part-time job? Or are you about to walk across that stage in the funny square hat with a silly expression that says "I'm lost?" The more time you have, the better you can prepare yourself financially for your educational future. Time will allow you to find employment, fill out scholarship applications, and explore your many options for college education. Conversely, lack of time forces you to lower standards, expectations and enable you to make decisions in haste, which often are the worst decisions of all.

So how much time do you have? Don't panic. If you have time (say, you are a junior or younger), it does not mean you can relax and put things off until next school year or the summer. Go out and get a job today and get paid. Get real paid. If, on the other hand, you can hear Pachelbel's Canon ringing in your ears, and suddenly realize that college is a summer away and you have no money saved, you may be fighting an uphill battle, but you can still win. And this book will show you how.

Whether university is days or years away, you can use the same, simple tool to get an understanding of how much funding you will have to pay for tuition, books, fees and living expenses. Simplest. Tool. Ever.

The Simplest Tool Ever for Figuring College Funding:

Funding Source	Amount
1) **Cash Money Yo** (this is physical cash you have in your wallet, in the piggy bank, under your mattress, etc.)	$_____
2) **Checking & Savings Accounts** (what you have in the bank)	$_____
3) **529 Education Plan** (ask your parents if they have one for you)	$_____
4) **Other Cash on Hand** (any other cash that is in your name)	$_____
TOTAL CASH ON HAND Add lines 1-4 to get your total Cash On Hand.	$_____
5) **Employment** (you can estimate how much you can realistically save from now until your first semester)	$_____
6) **Scholarships** (money that you have been or will be awarded)	$_____
7) **Grants** (money that you have been or will be awarded)	$_____
8) **Anticipated Money from Parents** (money that your parents have today that they promise to put towards your education.. Trips to Vegas and lottery tickets do not count)	$_____
9) **Anticipated Money from Grandparents** (money that your grandparents have today that they have promised to put towards your education. Ditto Vegas and lottery. Add Bingo.)	$_____
10) **Other Anticipated Money** (all other money that you have a reasonable expectation of receiving for college)	$_____
TOTAL ESTIMATED FUNDING Add Total Cash On Hand and lines 5-10 to get your Total Estimated Funding.	$_____

Your **Total Estimated Funding** is the amount that you should reasonably anticipate having at the start of your first semester. With this information, you can make more informed decisions about the colleges you should consider.

This tool is made simple so that it can be used over and over again. The amounts on each line will change, often from day to day, so it is worth your while to periodically check in and adjust the amount, at least so that you have in your mind a working number from which to base future decisions on.

One of the funding sources mentioned is the 529 Education Plan. This is simply a financial plan that your parents may have used to save money for you for college. Different states have varying rules on these education savings plans, but suffice it to say, if it is an account in which you are the benefactor, then you can consider it money available to you for college. Unfortunately, these financial plans are not often utilized by parents, for a host of reasons.

It is recommended that you find out how much money you might expect from your parents and/or grandparents. The earlier you figure out the realistic amount of financial aid from your family, the better you will be able to gauge yourself and your future prospects of universities. Also, the sooner you ask, the sooner your parents and grandparents might be able to set aside some money for you for college. If you understand early on that your family simply cannot afford to offer you any help, then you can make better-informed college choices, and certainly will not be shocked when the bill for fall tuition shows up with your name on it. Be honest with your family about this. They will most likely be honest with you. Look at the numbers realistically, not ideally. This figure may change, perhaps even significantly, between now and the time you leave for university. And if you suddenly learn that your parents don't have that education fund you always assumed they had, don't get upset. It's not really their responsibility to fund your college education. It's your responsibility. Are you still telling yourself "I can't wait to grow up?"

Go local.

Live on less money than you make. As soon as you can. As much as you can. Try to find a part-time job nearby. I say "nearby" because every trip you make and every mile you travel further from home costs you money and time, even if it pays a few dollars more per hour. True, a local job might not be the most glamorous job around, but it pays. Yes, your friends may see you in your fast food uniform asking them if they want fries with their order, but it pays money. It may not be fun, but it pays money. It may not even pay well, but it...you guessed it- pays money. Again, how much is your pride worth to you?

When I was in high school, many of my friends got jobs at an amusement park 35 miles from the small town where we lived. It was awesome - outside, in the sun, decent pay and perceivably glamorous work - but that's where the awesome stopped. The amusement park was 45 minutes away (when traffic wasn't bad), and the pay was only slightly over minimum wage. They averaged 15 hours a week. So every day these part-time workers had to drive 1.5 hours round trip, costing them time and gas money. The pay was slightly higher than most high school students, but was it really worth it? At the end of the month, those students who stayed in town and worked the humble jobs at the local grocery store, restaurant or shop went home with more money in their pocket. After all, they didn't have to pay for a tank of gas every other day, and they didn't lose two hours of working time commuting every day. Oh, I might also mention, the amusement park closed for a couple of months every winter, so those workers either had to find other employment, or temporary employment, or, as was the case most of the time, just sit around the house and wait until the park opened up in the spring. Those storm troopers weren't going to shoot themselves!

How much was their pride worth to them?

Commuter Chic		Hometown Humble	
$10/hour pay		$8/hour pay	
15 hours/week		20 hours/week	
35 mile, 45 minute commute		5 mile, 10 minute commute	
$10/hr x 15hrs/wk weekly	$150	$8/hr x 20 hrs/wk weekly	$160
35 miles = 1.75 gallons	-52.50	5 miles = .25 gallons	-7.50
Weekly Income:	**$97.5**	**Weekly Income:**	**$152.5**

Assumptions: vehicle gets 20 miles/gallon; gasoline costs $3/gallon, work 5 days/wk

After travel and time costs, the student working the "glamorous job" at the amusement park made over $50 a week less - except in the winter when the park was closed and they made nothing or had to find other employment. Had the worker stayed nearby, which likely meant working for less money, and spent an extra hour a day on the clock instead of commuting, then he or she would have actually made about $150 a week. *And had an extra 30 minutes to blast storm troopers!*

So for the amusement park workers with the awesome job, their pride was worth about $50 a week. It's not much, but it adds up. In a year, it adds up to about $2,600. Imagine what you could do with that. Save it, perhaps? Live on less money than you make. And if you budget your money well, and manage it wisely and not spend it frivolously, you might find yourself with quite the little chunk of change when you go off to college.

Now that you have a little money saved up, you should seriously consider, if you have not already done so, opening a bank account. This is a safe place to store your G's while you work to make more. Having a bank account sometimes helps you save your money, because your money is not where you are. And if your money is in a different location than the person who can spend it, then it is far less likely to be spent. Out of sight, out of mind. For some people, having cash helps them budget. Many of us are more emotionally attached to cold, hard cash. We feel its loss more than the simple swipe of plastic. Consequently, some people put most of their money into a bank account and keep a budgeted amount of cash in their pocket to limit spending. You have to be the judge of what's best for you.

Go national.

You may want to consider going to a larger national bank when you open your first bank account. Try to find one that has branches both near home and near the universities you are considering. This way, when and if you leave your town for college, you won't have to open another bank account there. It may not seem like a big deal, but it's one less headache to deal with during your first few weeks of school. Plus you will have the ability to withdraw money while at school, or at home, or traveling in between. If at least one of your parents is a joint holder of the account, then they can effectively deposit money in your bank account from home. Just make sure they don't withdraw!

When I was in college, I managed a rock band, and travelling on weekends all over the country meant access to my bank account became a problem in places. Having a national bank behind me really helped.

In the First Edition of this book, we used to discuss cell phone plans and laptops, because at the time, these were considerable expenses for college students. Today, while they are still pricey, they have become ubiquitous, and we often find ourselves heading off to State with a cell phone on our parents' phone plan and a 2 year old tablet. So while we won't go into details anymore on this subject, remember:

Don't go over your minutes or data.

Don't buy a laptop or tablet if the computer lab is open, and don't overspend - Students get deep discounts for most software.

Work a lot, if you can, and then work a lot more in the summer. Work as much as you can without sacrificing academics in high school. Good grades are important, too. With good grades, you make yourself more marketable and attractive to potential colleges. Universities all across the country are interested to know what your GPA and class rank are. They do not see that you did this while working part time, or spending every waking hour studying, or simply spending the day blasting storm troopers. They just see your GPA and academic performance, aptitude exam scores (SAT, ACT), extracurricular activities and other entrance requirements.

Get a head start.

Most high schools have programs where you can earn college credit for certain classes offered at your school. This is a great chance to take advantage of opportunities and save a lot of money and time after you start along your path towards a university degree. It is not uncommon for some high school students to earn an entire semester's worth of undergraduate course credit before they even decide which school they want to attend. Yes, these classes will more than likely require some extra homework and effort, but the payoff is great! If you were to take and pass one of these classes that count towards college credit, then you would save yourself the cost of tuition, any associated fees, and the cost of textbooks (my God, the cost of textbooks!). That's a lot of money! What if you were able to take enough of these classes to earn an entire semester's worth of credit? How much would you save? Or put another way, how much less debt would you have when you graduate college in a few years?

Some high schools do not offer these college credit courses, but they may have some type of fellowship program with a neighboring school district. If you have any questions regarding the details of your particular high school's programs, stop by your counselor's office and inquire.

Be aware that some of you may find it to your advantage not to take these courses for college credit. When you pass a high school course and receive the credit, you do not get a grade for the class - simply a "passed" mark to go on your transcript. For some students, it might be better to have taken the course in college and received a letter grade in the class (provided that you do well). For example, students who intend on going to medical school, where GPA is of paramount importance in the application materials, can find it advantageous to forego the potential college credit while in high school and take those courses while in college, where you get full credit for the grade and potentially boost your GPA. So if you're gunning for a post-grad degree that you know has very high entrance requirements, it might be best to take the "easy A" to boost your GPA, and make your candidacy for the post-grad school stronger. This is certainly an area where you should weigh the advantages and disadvantages against your particular situation. Talk it over with everyone around you, and make your best judgment. If you find that you made the wrong decision, do not waste anytime regretting it.

Many times you can do both – take all the college credit courses in high school that you can, and if you find yourself struggling in your undergraduate courses, retake one of those easy courses to get an A onto your transcript and boost the GPA.

There are a lot of things you can do to start preparing for college, and the sooner you start, the easier the path is going to be. Don't wait until the last minute - this isn't an English test where you forgot to read the book and at worst you can read the back cover to get an idea of what it is about. This is your life, your future. Why would you not make this your number one mission at this point? Or is Friday night out with the gang more important? You might lose some cool points, but you'll get them all back when you pass them on the road in your European sports car. How much is your pride worth to you?

2   CHOOSE THE MAJOR, THEN CHOOSE THE SCHOOL

Choosing your college is going to be one of the biggest decisions of your young life. Where you go to school will have a large impact on your grades, your degree and level of knowledge, your career path and how much you pay for your education. And your choice of school has even greater impact on your life than simply money and grades; many people meet their husband or wife in school. Some of you will have life-defining events as a result of where you attend college. Your first job and career may be affected by where you go to school. Even some of the smaller things in life will be affected, and you'd be quite surprised to learn just how much of your future life as an adult, as a spouse, and as a parent are influenced by the college you attend.

Would you like to hear a love story? I'll tell you mine very briefly. I chose a small college in central Texas for various reasons, one being that my family leased some land outside of the town and I enjoyed that I could escape from the world and study, relax, fish, or whatever else I wanted without interruption (note: this is not a reason to choose a college). The scholarships were available, and financially it appeared that I could afford to attend, even though it was a private university. So I moved to this little town. Proverbially, it was the middle of nowhere. Geographically, it was the middle of nowhere. At one point during my first semester I noticed an ad for a job during the summer at a camp near my hometown. So I applied, got the job (which was great because you work full time, and room and board were free), and ultimately worked five summers while I was in college (yes, it took me five years to graduate, but that's another story). My second summer I worked with the most enchanting woman I have ever met. She

11

was a young lady from abroad working through an exchange program. We dated, grew in love with one another, and eventually got married. Today, I see her playing with our two boys and am amazed to think that I would have never met the love of my life had I not worked at that summer camp where I wouldn't have worked had I not seen the ad at the school which I wouldn't have attended had my family not leased land in central Texas. Yes, you can argue fate, destiny, or whatever. But I'm glad I went; it has made all the difference.

You yourself might be making this choice very soon, and the repercussions of that decision will have a great impact on your future - in ways that you can't imagine. But do not be frightened - be excited! Who knows what surprises await you in this next big era of your unique life?

Your college degree will determine so much of your future career, earning potential and lifestyle that it almost seems unfair to place that burden on someone with limited experience and limited funds. But that's reality, and you will be seeing a lot more of it the older you get.

There are literally thousands of areas to study and specialize in as you go through your college years. Picking the one or two areas where you want to focus is daunting, but we can break it down into manageable decision-points. Consider the Venn diagram below (don't worry – you'll get to know all about Venn diagrams in college).

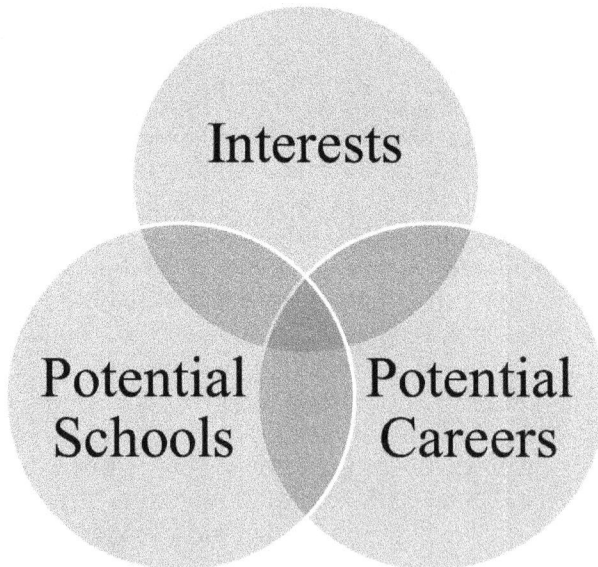

The ideal school and major will be at the confluence of your interests, the potential careers (and their respective earnings) and the schools that teach the knowledge to help you succeed in those interests and careers.

Consider your interests.

Think about what you are interested in – those things that you like to do when no one is telling you what to do. Specifically, what subjects in school are the most interesting to you? Which ones are you a natural at? Could you do something for the rest of your life in that area? If it helps, write them down.

Consider your career potential.

Next, consider the careers available to you if you were an expert in your areas of interest. Is your passion drawing? What jobs are available to people who are great at drawing? What do they earn? Is it something that you could simply keep as a hobby, and focus on an area of interest that has more career potential? Ask your parents and other people whom you trust to mentor you with this list. They will have a larger array of experience to advise you with. So long as you listen.

As an exercise, my father asked me when I was young what I wanted to do for fun when I grew up. Go hiking? Play guitar? Race cars? Did I want a big house on 500 acres of land, or a condo in the city? Did I want a sexy exotic sports car? Did I care not what I drove? Did I like traveling abroad or traveling to the next state? It took me a while to answer, because I had not pondered that when I was young. But once I had some idea, he started assigning dollars to each "goal" I had when I was an adult. Have a home? That cost $200,000 in the city near where I lived. Travel overseas each year for a couple of weeks? I needed to make at least $3,000 more annually to support my fun. Drive a Porsche? That costs money too. And then he started asking about kids, and family, and retirement, and taxes! My head was spinning!

But it was a good exercise. The realization that striving for the lifestyle I wanted required a career that supported it really helped me focus my attention on my career choices, and the need for it to hold my interests.

Then I needed to find the right school to educate me on those interests and set me up for the right career.

Consider the schools.

With the knowledge of what life I wanted to live as an adult, and a rough idea of the amount of income I needed to earn to support that, I set about finding a career that I was interested in that also paid enough for me to enjoy life. Personally, I loved to draw, but I decided that none of the careers that paid well that involved drawing were for me. I considered engineering, where one drafts up an idea for a new pump, or building support, or whatever, and then uses one's drawing skills to illustrate, or communicate, the design to others. None of those jobs interested me, so I moved drawing out of the career opportunity column to simply a hobby, which I still enjoy.

Eventually I decided on an area of interest that held many career options that, by and large, paid well, and I was passionate about. The next step was to find the right school to set me up for a great career. And that's what you can do as well. Once you have a short list (in your head, written down – whatever works best for you) of your interests and the careers that will support your interests and the lifestyle you want to lead, the next step is finding the best school to set you up for success.

One way to do this is by going to published lists. Several magazines and news companies offer endless lists of top schools and other institutions for your ranking pleasure. While the ethics of the lists may be questionable (in some instances, colleges pay to be on the list, which opens the door to collusion and other corrupt acts) the fact remains that employers take note of which colleges are generally mentioned from many of these lists. These are people and firms that may hire you when you graduate, so it is worthwhile getting to know who they notice.

Another way is simply asking your parents, mentors, teachers and other people with more life experience than you, which schools they think are best, especially for your area of interest. In Texas, I was told great engineers came from a particular school within the state, but that unofficially the best engineers came from a local school that wasn't as well-known. If I were planning to live locally after graduating, I was advised, I was better off going to the local school. Anything outside of the metropolitan area I lived in, and I was better off going to the better-known school. Great advice.

If you are planning to be a professor, then a different set of rules apply to you. For academics, it matters not what the national magazines and news outlets rank, but what the academic community views as the best schools (which often translate to mean the best professors). So if you're pursuing an academic route to one day become a professor, then you must choose the schools with the professors who are top in their particular field. More on that later.

For most of us, our choices of universities are greatly narrowed by the college admission process. In other words, much of the determining factor is going to be who takes us and who doesn't. Not everyone gets accepted to every school. In fact, not everyone will get into your local state university. Please understand that this is nothing personal, and by no means are you a failure if you do not get into the school that you wish to go to. Colleges set up their admission guidelines to look for particular "blends" of students to comprise their student body. And every college has a different set of standards than the rest. Some place a higher emphasis on your graduating GPA. Others really look at your SAT or ACT scores, or both. Some even want to know your attendance record (uh huh- now you're probably wishing you would have stayed in school on Senior Skip Day). Most colleges look at the whole picture, meaning your grades, your attendance, your test scores (even your conduct), and make their determination from there. And the more popular the school is to attend, the more guidelines will be set up to limit those that enroll every semester. This is not to get rid of the "bad" kids, and you are by no means one if you are not accepted to any particular university. It is simply done to keep the student population at a manageable level and at the right mix to support social, economic and cultural growth.

You should ideally start thinking about where you would like to go for college sometime during your sophomore year of high school. If you are already a senior, it's crunch time. You're not going to be out of time, but you're certainly not going to have a lot of it, especially with keeping your grades up in school, and going through all of the senior hoop-la. During your junior year, you should start narrowing your options down to a dozen or so colleges. By the time your senior year is well underway, you should generally have a pretty good idea of a few colleges that seem to really grab your attention. And by the time you graduate high school, you should already be accepted and admitted to the college that you plan to attend in the fall.

So which college is best for you? Like a good pair of jeans, colleges come in all shapes and sizes, but there is usually only one or two that fit you perfectly. Your mission is to determine which school is the best school for you. A combination of factors go into this, such as your current choice on a future career, school size and notoriety, location, and very importantly, cost.

First, let's look at those big state universities whose logo everyone wears on their baseball caps and XXL sweatshirts. Because they are usually partially funded by the state (i.e. the taxes your parents pay every year), and because of the sheer number of students attending , the cost is more than likely going to be more affordable than alternatives such as private school . By no means does this mean that attending this type of school is going to be cheap- there's no such thing as "cheap education."

Large, state-funded universities1 offer several advantages over smaller and/or private schools. They typically offer more majors, more electives, more local attractions, more people to meet, more familiarity with potential future employers, and importantly, a larger alumni association.

Changes of major is extremely common in college, and if you decide you no longer want to pursue your original area of study, changing a major does not necessarily mean changing the university. In fact, the average college student changes his or her major three times by the time they graduate. That's not a bad thing: in a certain light, finding yourself is as much a part of the college experience as obtaining the diploma.

Big universities also come with larger departments and more esteemed faculty. This correlates into the potential for gaining a very rich understanding of your particular field of interest. In other words, there's more brain per major. You may find yourself learning under some rather noteworthy professors, some of them leading experts in their field. If you befriend these men and women, you will have access to much more opportunities than you would at a smaller, lesser known university. It may mean something as trivial as the offer of a different viewpoint on a matter, but it could mean big things - it looks great on a resume. What if you could say in a future job interview that you studied under Albert Einstein, or Carl Sagan? There are some people alive today who can say that.

---

[1] It should be noted that "state-funded" schools derive less and less funds from the state, which means more and more of the cost burden is being shifted to students. This is a large driver of regular and sizeable increases in tuition and other fees at state universities.

Aside from the academic, big colleges and universities can offer a lot of other attractions. There are chances to travel abroad and study overseas. This, too, can look good on your resume, especially if you want to work for a large, multi-national corporation.

The nightlife can be a lot of fun, as long as it doesn't get out of hand. Big universities are located in big towns, so there will always be plenty of places to go and things to do. Whether it be a unique local hangout or a big amusement park, you'll never be at a loss for something to entertain yourself (and often inexpensively).

There are also greater chances for employment with larger towns, so you can never lay that lame excuse on your parents that "there are just no jobs around here."

Finally, with big schools, the very name itself can take you places after you graduate. This really comes in handy when applying and interviewing for a job. A hiring manager may have had great success with several alumni of a big school, whereas with a smaller school they may either not know it, or may have a lower opinion of the quality of education you received because of a single graduate previously hired from that school who underperformed. Conversely, that single graduate may be a stellar employee and help sway the hiring manager to consider you, though you be from a smaller university.

There are disadvantages of the big universities, however, and they are many. First, in a big school, you really get the impression that you cannot stand out. Teachers may often literally refer to you as a number, and you certainly enroll, sign up for classes, and get credits as a number. It can seem like nobody cares who you are at larger universities, or what your dreams are or what you hope to do with your life. It's nothing personal - they simply have too many students, and not enough time to take interest in every person who walks through the gates of the school.

It is very hard to distinguish yourself academically, as well. The more students there are, the harder a professor - especially freshman level courses - may try and fail you. The reasons for this are simple – for one, getting students to drop out of courses reduces their workload as professors. Second, the school already has your money, at least for the first semester, and they simply cannot sustain the sheer numbers of freshman students all the way through to senior level courses. Financially, schools would love it. Practically, the facilities cannot support it. So it is necessary to weed out those that don't have what it takes from those that do. You may find yourself in a classroom of 200 students your freshman year, but by the time you are a senior, your classes are drastically smaller - say, 25 students. And that senior level course may be the only one offered that particular semester, whereas there are ten or so freshman level classes in the same course. So your freshman year you find yourself doing battle not with storm troopers, but with the guy who spent his time studying. The storm troopers don't look so deadly now. No, it's the quiet guy in the desk next to you with a personalized graphing calculator who threatens to take over your world.

Do you remember that big schools are in big towns, with big things to do? This can also be a drawback, especially if you are overly enticed by the nightlife and entertainment. Many a good student has lost his or her way because they became too distracted by all of the hoopla of college towns. Yes, there is always something to do, but do not catch yourself always doing something. And with more distractions, there are more chances for you to lose your money - a very scarce commodity when trying to get your degree. The moral of the story is, if you know you like to gamble, don't go to a school located next to a casino. If you know you cannot handle prioritizing school over fun, then you should seriously consider commuting from home, or attending a smaller school in a smaller town with fewer attractions ...er…distractions.

Throughout my four years of high school, I noticed that all of the students who went to a particular university in my state did not finish the first semester. Every one of them dropped out – each for different specific reasons, but generally speaking, it was too great of a jump for them to go from their home environment to a city with more people, more distractions, tougher classes and no parental oversight. For a few, it was their first real exposure to drugs and other substances, and the temptation got the best of them. Given this observation, I opted not to go to this school, to avoid the same risk of failure that my peers did. Pity – it is a great school with a large alumni population, and a great network for job hunting.

Smaller universities offer a different experience altogether. Both good and bad, the journey is definitely not the same as a large state university. Generally speaking, smaller universities offer fewer majors, so there might be fewer opportunities to explore other study areas during your college tenure. Consequently, changing majors might not be a plausible option to you unless you find that you like one of the limited areas that the smaller university offers.

Many smaller universities are located in smaller cities, so attractions (distractions?) are fewer. For some, this is a good thing, as the many things to do around town can usurp the necessary things to do in class. At the same time, for those of us who can excel in class and be adventurous with the world around us, a larger city might offer more satisfaction. For my undergraduate degree, I attended a small school in a small town, and regularly found myself getting out of town on weekends, holidays and just about any opportunity I could. My parents worried a bit at the fact I was putting 25,000 miles a year on my auto, with none of those miles used to commute to school and work. True, many smaller universities exist in large metropolitan areas, and for many, this is perhaps the best of both worlds. Know thyself, and know thy maturities and limitations.

One major factor of smaller universities (and they are happy to market this to you) is class size. Typically, classes are smaller and, while it might not be a big deal when you're in high school, it can become a big deal in college. I used to have this mantra I would tell myself:

Smaller classes = better grades

While there is no empirical correlation between the two, I have indeed found that to be the case for myself and many students across the US. It is not that you will receive a letter grade higher than you normally would by simply attending with fewer students. Rather, smaller classes often put students in environments where they can ask questions, or feel a stronger connection with the professor, and thus the material being taught. There are, no doubt, several studies that elucidate this, but suffice it to say, you might achieve a higher GPA in college if you seek out smaller classes. And by the way, you can find smaller classes at large universities, too!

With smaller classes comes one of the best opportunities that exist with college – getting to know your professors! There are many advantages to building relationships with your professors. If you actively participate in class, they will often take a more vested interest in your learning of the material. It might mean adding a few extra minutes onto their presentations to make sure you understand the subject. It might mean giving you the benefit of the doubt on a borderline answer to an exam question (trust me; this has happened to me more times than I can count). After finishing their courses, it might mean getting a letter of recommendation or a referral to a very rewarding summer internship or first job. It might mean an insider's track on what other professors to take, or what courses to take that would make you stand out among other graduates. In sum, get to know your professors! There is no downside except a little of your time.

Another large difference that a person will notice traveling from a large campus to a small campus is the personal interest that people take in you and your well-being. In fact, the first impression I got of the school I eventually graduated from was when a complete stranger, noticing that I was new and a bit lost (you know - the deer caught in the headlights look), stopped and asked if I needed any help. It really meant a lot, and the impression is still there, years later (thanks Sanch: you taught me more about human kindness than any Business Ethics 101 could ever hope to). In smaller universities, you can really feel like a valued person, and not just another number. Larger universities have caught onto this as well, and you may find many efforts by big campuses to treat each "school" (School of Engineering, School of Fine Arts, e.g.) as a mini-college with programs and activities designed to encourage that small group inclusion in the midst of a many thousand-strong campus.

There are some drawbacks to smaller schools, however, and you should certainly take these into account when choosing your future alma mater. You may lack the opportunities at a smaller school to study under great professors. Though small schools have some very talented professors, they may not be well-known or have a Nobel Prize hanging over their fireplace at home. This might not be a big deal now, but if you have any intention of staying in academia, your professor matters.

Often (and with many exceptions) smaller universities can cost more than larger universities, for a variety of reasons. If they are private, the university likely does not receive funds from the state, so they must make up for that lost funding source through other sources, and that often ends up being you, the student. Even public universities that are smaller often receive less in funding from the state and, having a smaller alumni population, typically receive less donations and endowments. Again, financial shortcomings are often laid at the feet of students to cover. There are many exceptions to this rule, so do your due diligence when considering the universities, and be well aware of the costs of each, so you know what you are getting into before you pack your bags in August.

One of the biggest drawbacks of smaller universities is name recognition. While some small universities have worldwide recognition, most are obscure. Big universities, often with big sports programs, have big alumni populations who support their school and are well-known throughout the

US. This can make your job search much easier after you graduate. While few people will tell you officially, unofficially,

Alumni tend to hire from their Alma Mater.

So, the more alumni there are, the more opportunities exist for you to get hired onto your first job. Keep this in mind as you are making your school choices.

Graduating from a small college, I struggled when I graduated. Moving to a large city, my obscure little university was not well-known, and consequently my resume was not given much value compared to other applicants from larger schools. Whatever the reason, if the school is little known, little value is assigned. Even once I was hired into a career-building role, I found myself earning almost 10% less than my big campus, big sports program peers. If all you have on your resume is your school and your major, it makes a difference at the interview table. I found this to be true today, even when I am doing the hiring. Recently I interviewed a candidate with an MBA (Masters of Business Administration) from a school I had never heard of before, located 40 miles from the town I grew up in, and immediately I discounted it as an MBA of no significant value. This candidate might have been my best hire, but her education, along with a few items discussed in the interview, did not make her stand out among the other candidates.

So as you are comparison shopping universities, consider the notoriety of the university as much as you consider the cost. If comparing a couple of options and one university might cost a little more but offer a lot more name recognition, then (all other things being equal) it is worth considering the more recognizable school.

Attend in state.

Unless you're rich (in which case why are you reading this book?) there is a high penalty paid by students (and their parents) to attend universities in other states. It's called out-of-state tuition, and if that school does not offer significant scholarships to offset out-of-state tuition costs, then staying within your state may be the best option.

Moreover, as an out of state student you will be ineligible to receive state approved funding such as grants and scholarships because of your residency status, meaning that if you live in California and you attend school in Florida, you will likely find that you don't qualify for state financial aid from your home state because you are attending school somewhere else, and you won't qualify for state financial aid from your university's state because you are not a resident there.

If you attend out of state, move.

One way to get around some of the out-of-state tuition costs is by investigating a school's in-state rule requirements. Typically they require having a "permanent address" within the state for a set number of months (typically 12 months, which prevents you from moving to a permanent address the summer before school starts. Those bastards.). This is when you can get creative. Do you have any family or close friends living in the state where you want to go to school? Maybe it's time to start cozying up to them. At least a year out from college, draw up a rental contract and rent a room in their house for, say, $50 a month. Then you have the documented proof in the form of copies of checks and the rental agreement to prove you have been living in that state for the past year. Go further and change your driver's license, your taxes, anything. Consider it that you have moved to that state and are only temporarily living with your parents back home. Call it underhanded. Call it unethical. Call it what you will. You can also call it money in the bank for next semester's tuition.

You might also call the out-of-state school you wish to attend and see if there are any incentives for waiving the out-of-state tuition. Some schools do not charge the higher rates for incoming freshmen who have a certain ACT or SAT score, or if a student is ranked high in his or her class.

Play in the minors before getting called up to the big league.

Consider community college for your first year of college. While it is not glamorous, it cuts cost considerably. Now, before you slam this book down in a screaming fit, please take an honest look at this option. And remember how much your pride is worth to you. Many of us, myself included, want so badly to tell our friends how we've been accepted to NYU and we're going to go there, take acting classes, get a job on Broadway and then make a huge break into movies. Or we want to say that we're going to an Ivy League school where tuition is only for the super-rich or super-connected. Consider this: employers don't care where you started school. The only care where you graduate from.

If you consider going to a small (and local) college your first year, you might be able to cut considerable costs out of the total education funding requirements. Just ensure (and this is a big one) that each course you take will transfer equally to any of the colleges you are considering. That's often a lot of phone calls before the start of each semester, and a lot of emails confirming. But it could save you thousands.

As an example, we grabbed three random schools of higher education – a private university, a state university, and a community college. The fees break down like this:

Type of School	Semester Tuition	Activity Fees	Other Fees	TOTAL
Private University	$4,950	$275	$125	$5,350
State University	$1,975	$225	$75	$2,275
Community College	$725	$75	$75	$875

What a difference! By staying at a community college for a year, you could save $2,800! If you went to a private university after a year at community college you could save almost $9,000! With those kinds of savings, you could walk across the stage at graduation with your diploma and straight into a brand new convertible. And this comparison does not include living costs. So, if you can, go to local community college first and knock out those core classes. And if you can do it while staying at home, all the better.

One thing you should not do is choose your school based upon where your friends are going, or where your girlfriend or boyfriend is going. I know, I know, you're thinking "I'll go where he/she is going, and soon we will get married, and have 2.3 kids, 1.3 cars, and live in that little house down the lane with the white picket fence and rose garden, and we'll have great jobs and the kids will always mind their manners and make good grades in school and my spouse and I will grow old together with smiles on our faces and blah blah blah ...."

Reality check - the vast majority of people do not marry their high school sweetheart, and for good reason: there is so much more maturity needed that many lack when in high school. You need to have that time away from parents and boyfriends and girlfriends and other crutches to lean on so that you can learn to be self-reliant. We'll discuss marriage issues in detail later.

So please ...PLEASE!!! ...do not base your choice of college on friends or who you're dating. Step back and look at the big picture, and make the choice that's best for you. Very quickly you will see that you are happier where you belong, and your sweetheart is happier where they belong.

Where you go to college is a choice that ultimately is made by you. You can go where your friend or date goes, or where your parents push you, or where your favorite college basketball team plays. Or you could look at all of the choices you have and make the decision that is best for you and you alone. No one can make this decision for you. It is yours to make. Welcome to the responsibilities (and joys) of adulthood. Choose carefully, and choose wisely. Later on, down that road less traveled, you can smile and see that it indeed made all the difference.

3   GRANTS & LOANS

According to some reports, millions of dollars of money for education - in the form of scholarships, grants, company reimbursement plans and the like - go unclaimed each year, simply because people don't know that it's there. Your parents will think of it as their tax dollars finally at work for something they can use. You can think of it as the secret level where you can rack up a bunch of points and 1ups, and you can have access to the goods if you know the right passwords. I'm about to give you those passwords.

Sources of these lesser-known funds include Federal and state government agencies, private foundations, special awards, and the like. Some grants are based on religion, race, ethnic background, last name, gender, physical disabilities, parents' job, even hobbies (you may consider writing to professional associations pertaining to your specific skills or interests, just to establish connections or memberships that you can include in scholarship applications later). I've even seen a scholarship that qualified persons who "look physically fit" though there are some serious ethical issues with that one.

FEDERAL PROGRAMS

An abundance of help for education is available through a number of grant and loan programs run by the U.S. Department of Education and its subsidiary agencies. Most colleges and universities participate in federal programs that provide various amounts of funding for tuition, housing, and other school-related expenses. Often the schools directly administer the disbursements, and the students apply directly to the financial aid office. Federal financial aid typically comes in 3 forms:

1) Grants - which do not have to be repaid.
2) Subsidized Loans - for which the federal government pays the interest until schooling ends.
3) Unsubsidized Loans - for which the student incurs the interest charges while in school, but payment of the charges may be deferred until school is completed.

PELL GRANTS

Pell grants are outright gifts to undergraduates who do not have a degree. Outright gifts - as in the money does not have to be paid back. Did you catch that?

You do not have to pay back a grant!

It is as if the government gives you a scholarship, just for being you. So it is these types of funding you should seek first when looking for federal money. That's why I mention this first. Remember it- there's a quiz on this later.

Pell grants are available to needy students based on a formula that takes into consideration your income and assets, your family's income and assets, home or farm equity, family size, etc. Under the most recent federal spending bill from Washington, the maximum annual award is now $5,815, with the highest awards given to families who have the greatest financial need.

For further information about Pell Grants or any other federal student aid program, talk to your high school counselor or the college financial aid office, or look at

https://studentaid.ed.gov

FEDERAL SUPPLEMENTAL EDUCATIONAL OPPORTUNITY

GRANTS (FSEOG)

These grants are intended for students with exceptional financial need. They are generally for smaller dollar amounts than the typical Pell Grant, averaging between $100 and $4000 per year. But $100 is always better than $0. So do not frown upon these smaller grants. Every little bit helps.

The way this program works is different than Pell Grants in that the federal government gives the money to participating schools (so find out if your school is participating before pursuing this any further). These schools, in turn, grant the money to students to supplement other funds that they might be receiving. If you are getting Pell Grants, you will receive a higher priority than those who do not. It's nice to be at the front of the line! And unlike student loans, which we will discuss next, FSEOGs do not have to be repaid. Do I need to write that again or have you caught it? Oh, why not:

You do not have to pay back a grant!!!

Have you caught it by now?

STAFFORD GUARANTEED STUDENT LOANS

This program is the main program employed by the U.S. government in regards to educational assistance on a federal level (that's a lengthy way of saying this is your easiest shot at money for college). Traditionally almost 40% of all students in America use this program, and there is a good reason for it - a manageable interest rate, not to mention federal backing. Yes, some of you are wondering how a government entity with over a trillion dollars of ballooning debt can guarantee any amount of money, but don't look at me for the answer. I just tell you how it is. If you really want an intelligent, though wordy answer, call your Congressional representative. Do you know their names? You should, because they almost certainly do not know you.

Students using this program borrow money from a bank or private lender, and the federal government guarantees to pay back the loan in case the student defaults on the payments.

The downside of this type of assistance is that yes, you do have to pay the money back. But the upside is that the interest rate is typically lower than many other forms of borrowing. Also, under this program you don't have to start making payments on the loan until you've been out of college for 6-12 months, so there is at least a small window of time for you to "get out there and get a job." Damn - there goes that 2-year backpacking trek through Europe. Better make it a 3 day camping trip on your grandparent's farm. But take heart – laws are changing the way these loans are administered after graduation. Hardships can delay that day of reckoning further, or payments can be adjusted based upon income. Many other options exist, so you may yet make that backpacking trek after all.

There are two types of Stafford Loans - Subsidized and Unsubsidized. Either type employs the same rules concerning repayment of the loan starting a certain number of months after graduation. And this is assuming that a student remains full time. If you drop to part time status or drop out altogether then the clock starts ticking. And the loan must be repaid usually within ten years. This is a very important detail to consider. If you borrow $4,000 and you have 10 years to repay it, then your payment will not be quite so bad, and if you double up on some of the payment s and get the loan paid off sooner, then you will save money that would have gone to pay interest. On the other hand, if you borrow $30,000 to go to that prestigious private school that got you the very same job as the community college grad, you still have only ten years to repay the loan. Therefore your payments are going to be substantially higher, and you will pay more in interest over the long term. The moral of the story is to take out as few, if any loans as you possibly can, and pay the brunt of your college expenses through scholarships and - dare I say it - employment. Is that a dirty word?

The difference between the two types of loans translates into dollar signs out of your pocket. Subsidized loans are set up so that the government actually pays the interest while you are in school. But there is a catch (isn't there always a catch?). You have to exhibit financial need to qualify for this specific type of loan.

Unsubsidized loans accrue interest the entire time you are in school. So in the long run you will pay more money back than with a subsidized loan, but these loans are more readily available. There are no financial need requirements to get these types of loans, so they are available to anyone.

There are also some special circumstances in which you can have part or all of a loan forgiven - such as enlisting in the military, National Guard or reserves. Some programs exist for teachers working in special areas, such as inner city schools or the handicapped. You may also be able to find private enterprises and businesses who offer to pay off part of your student debt as part of their hiring package. You just have to ask around before you graduate about where these companies are and how you go about getting these debts forgiven or paid for you.

STAFFORD LOANS FOR PARENTS

Called Direct PLUS, there is a program by which parents of college students can take out loans for their (dependent) children's education. Under this plan, the parents must repay the loans. There are some other drawbacks to this type of financial assistance. First, the interest rate is somewhat higher than a typical loan taken out by the students themselves. And parents can usually only borrow the dollar amount equal to what the student owes after all other forms of financial aid have been considered. This is to keep parents from borrowing funds at low interest rates to, say, buy a boat.

PERKINS LOANS

This type of loan is for students with exceptional financial need. Often recipients of these types of loans also get other loans from various sources, and the Perkins Loan is simply to help cover additional college expenses that may exist. The interest rate is very low, and applications are made through the university itself, who collects the money from the government and lends it to the student. Like the Stafford Loans, payment on the loan begins 6-12 months after graduation or if a student drops to part time status or drops out altogether. Also, as before, there is a ten year period within which the student must repay the loan.

Just because these loans are meant for students with "exceptional need" doesn't necessarily mean that you will not get it if you have some funds coming in to help you pay for school. By all means apply every chance you can. The worst they can do is deny you the funds. The best they can do is reward you with upwards of $4000 a year, and by the time this book goes to press, that number might be even higher. But remember, you will have to pay all of it back.

There are also state funds appropriated for financial assistance to those who need it, or as is often the case, for those who apply. Check with your state's educational agencies to see what other types of loans are out there.

4   SCHOLARSHIPS

Major university seeks self-starter for data entry.

Part time, $50 hourly. Set own schedule.

Benefits include college degree without debt.

Great opportunity for growth.

Do you remember you first job? Those were the days, weren't they? Sweeping floors, mopping bathrooms, cleaning up that huge mess left by one of those supposedly wealthy families in your hometown (it makes you wonder that if they are so rich and sophisticated, how can they leave a table that is so messy a stray dog wouldn't touch it?). How much were you making? Minimum wage? Barely above?

Let's do an experiment. Go and ask your parents (you know, those old, boring people wearing clothes that were, like, so last decade, and that boss you around telling you not to stay out too late and wash behind your ears and take out the trash and mow the lawn and clean your room and .....) an honest question. And ask for an honest answer. How much does the average educated adult with a good paying job make an hour, by rough estimate? Got it? Good. You'll find that an individual with a decent paying job - say, $50,000 a year salary - working 40 hours a week makes around $24 an hour before paying the dreaded tax man.

Would you like to know an inside secret about how to make more than twice that per hour, and only do it part time?

You can earn about $50 an hour filling out scholarship applications.

In other words, the amount of time you spend filling out scholarship application forms compared to the average amount of money you get back equates to around $50 an hour. Put another way, the average professional pulling $100K a year working 60 hours a week (higher paid professionals often work more for their money) is working for around $43 an hour, and you will be pulling down more.

So with that said, you should be spending every spare moment of every evening (yes, even Friday nights if need be) filling out application after application for scholarships. The return for the work you put in is too great not to take advantage of. So, where to start looking for college cash?

First, let's make sure we're hunting for the same treasure. Let's recap the funding sources discussed at the beginning of this book.

Student loans. With student loans, you are applying with some form of lender (a large company who is in the business of making money) who will loan you the money for a time, but eventually you will have to pay the full amount back, along with some amount of interest. We will discuss some of the advantages and disadvantages of this later.

Grants. These are funds issued by the government, be it local, state or national, for use to pay college tuition. These are monetary funds that are given to you, and you do not have to pay them back. While there is a lot of money to be found here, the competition is fierce and the selection process arduous.

Family and friends. Parents never want to dish out large sums of hard-earned income to something they cannot immediately see, but they do love you (even when you got caught stealing road signs) and they want what's best for you and they understand that a college education will give you a head start in life so that you won't have to work as hard as they did to make a living. So they are willing to help you out with what they can. They might have a 529 Education Fund set up for you. They might have a stock portfolio, or an extra car they can sell, or some other asset that they can liquidate and turn into cash. But never expect them to finance your education.

You. Yes, you. There is certainly nothing wrong with taking your future seriously and going out yourself and raising the money through work (yes, I know it's a four-letter-word, but you're going to have to do this for the vast majority of your life). The earlier you start the more money you can save to apply towards college expenses.

The main focus of this section is on scholarships. They are monetary contributions awarded to a student. Scholarships are similar to grants in that they are money that you don't have to pay back. Generally, the term "grants" are used to describe government funds and "scholarships" are used to describe non-government funds, such as those given by private companies and other organizations. It is this type of funding that I want to focus on in this section, as this is your best chance of finding the free money you need to go to school.

The best place to begin your search for scholarships is in your own school. Go to your counselor, assistant principal, or if you are unsure, simply ask the people at the school's front desk where to go to inquire about scholarships. Typically this would be the non-teaching professional working for your educational district but your particular school might have someone else in charge of this area. Whoever it may be, they are often the best place to start in your quest for college money. The reason for this is simple - if they are good at their duties, they will have a wealth of knowledge and will direct you down the paths that you need to take. They will not know of every scholarship for which you would be available for, but they certainly will know what local scholarships are being offered and might very well have the application forms in their office.

Local scholarships are great sources of money and often your surest bet for getting those precious G's to slap down on the tuition table. Why local, you ask? Because the competition is the least fierce. You have to understand, while there are thousands of scholarships available to you, many of them are available to national applicants - meaning that you will be competing against that bookworm in Honors Physics from some town you've never heard of who has SAT scores and grades good enough to get a free ride at Princeton. But local scholarships greatly narrow the playing field. They are given out by local enterprises, usually to local students. Instead of competing against hundreds to thousands of students, you are simply competing against those students in your town or county who have taken the time to fill out an application. You may be one in 20 applicants rather than one in 20,000.

By no means should you count out national scholarships. After all, someone has to get them, and you can't win if your hat isn't in the ring. But playing the odds, you have a much better chance of getting awarded a local scholarship than a national one, so it's important to start off with a safer bet. You'll get to those big national scholarships later. So fill out those forms. Picking them up from your school's financial aid department doesn't mean squat. You won't get a dime unless you have an application completely filled out and in the hands of the person or persons who decide who gets their money.

One of the attributes of small towns is the fact that everybody knows everybody else. Do you have any idea how this equates into dollar signs? It means that if you're applying for a scholarship from a local business, then you can greatly increase your chances of getting that money by being noticed by that local business. Go down to the actual place of business, if you know they have the forms, and ask them for an application. Or better yet, ask for the store manager and introduce yourself, and then ask him or her for a scholarship application form. This will put a face to a name on that application form and score some serious brownie points when it comes time for the decision makers to make a decision on whom to give the money to. It may even be the only difference between your getting the money and the next person getting the money.

Larger metro areas offer a different scholarship hunting environment. More businesses and larger economic heft mean there may be more and larger scholarships available. But keep in mind that there are also more students searching for these scholarships.

Sometimes it is simply your last name that makes a difference. When I was young my father was trying to get into a particular post-grad school at a major university. He was applying from out of state and schools normally only allow a certain number of students to enroll from out of state. The selection process is very thorough, and when the dust settled he was selected a "runner-up" to get in. The gentleman who was selected immediately over my father had worse exam scores, a lower GPA, and much worse attendance records than my father. So my father inquired, and after a lot of beating around the bush by the admissions chief, my dad cornered him for a flat out answer. The man finally admitted that the man they selected over him was the nephew of one of the state senators. I'll let you in on an axiom you will find over and over again throughout your life:

It's not always what you know- it's who you know.

Eventually the man selected over my father dropped out and my dad enrolled. And all was well and there was a valuable lesson learned from the experience.

So how can you apply this lesson learned? Get together with your parents and see if they have any strings they can pull to help your chances in getting a scholarship. Your mom or dad may know someone who knows someone who owes someone else a favor. All you have to do is pull the right strings and bad-a-bing! You've got an in on the situation and can score big time. You might not. But you might. The only guarantee I can give you in your search for scholarships is that if you do nothing, you'll get nothing.

You and your parents might be surprised to find that their employer actually has a scholarship fund for their employees' students and - lo and behold - has some weight in the decision as to who gets the free money that they're handing out. True, some families have more connections than others, and your situation will be unique to every other graduating senior, but this is a huge stone to look under.

What strings do you have to pull? If you're working, ask your supervisor, human resource department, or manager to see what funding your employer may provide. Often with larger companies there are many scholarships available just for their employees who are attending college. This greatly reduces the number of competitors for the same money, thus improving your odds of getting some serious cash. Use your connections as a good employee (provided that you are one) to get money for college. Ask your parents to do the same thing. It's called the "good-ole-boy network," and while many bemoan it and how unfair it is, if you have the one, use it. Your education is on the line.

Scholarships are free money and free money is definitely for you.

Start your scholarship search by recruiting your parents, friends and family to the task. Get them thinking early and often about whom they know and what they know to help find that sweet, sweet college dough. Communicate regularly with them on where you stand, the cost of the college you would like to attend and the gap you need to make up.

Next, set a meeting with the person(s) in your school designated to help with college-related things. This may be a counselor, an assistant principal or other leader within your school. But each school, officially or unofficially, has at least one person who is the go-to expert on colleges, rankings, scholarships, majors, degrees and everything else related to secondary education. Ask them for every scholarship application they have. My school's counselor kept a very nice compendium of scholarships that, while at times containing outdated information was extremely helpful in identifying many national scholarships for which I could apply.

Sometimes there are scholarships with vague requirements or in many cases you meet all requirements except one.

When in doubt, apply anyway.

The worst they can do to you is say no. The best thing they can do is award you the scholarship because, despite missing a requirement or two, you were still the best applicant. You have nothing to lose, and everything to gain. So complete the applications and submit them ASAP.

Third, apply online with the Free Application for Federal Student Aid (FAFSA). This is the front door to most of the Pell Grants and federal student loans available to US students. Be aware that this often requires several key pieces of information, including recent tax returns. If you are listed as a dependent on your parent's most recent tax return (if you live at home with either or both of your parents, most likely you are) then you will need to provide information from their tax return as well.

www.fafsa.ed.gov

The FAFSA is critical to complete because outside of the federal loans, grants and other programs, some scholarship applications request copies of your FAFSA form.

Applying for scholarships is a never-ending task. It's like an extra piece of homework each night that you have to do. Except in this case, the reward for completing it is cold, hard cash for college. You will become sick of writing your name and demographic information on dozens upon dozens of forms. Just do it. The reward is greater than the pain.

Also, you will likely find many scholarship applications asking you to write a one page essay on some subject, usually why you are the best candidate for the scholarship, or what you want to do with your college studies. This is where a little up front effort pays off in efficiency later. Most of these scholarships ask for something along the lines of your future plans for school and career. Take the time to write your best article on this subject, and be very specific. For example, proclaim your interest in your particular subject area of choice, and include not only how passionate you are about the knowledge area, but what career you will pursue to match that passion. Then include the school, if applicable, that you plan on attending, and why it is the university best suited to prepare you for that career. Cite specific data points, like the growth in demand for people with the skills that you are seeking. About three specifically referenced points of fact will do, interspersed throughout the essay. What you are attempting to show is that you are passionate about a particular subject, and simultaneously realistic about how you will go about pursuing your passion. The message you're telling the person on the other end reviewing your essay versus the next essay is "I have a direction that I want to go, and I know how to get there."

Make it a great essay – a guaranteed A in any English class. Have others proofread it, and ask them to suggest any edits. Take their advice if it makes sense. Once you have your first-rate essay, you can repurpose it to other scholarship applications asking more or less the same thing. Change a sentence here or there to cater it to the specific essay question, but save yourself the work of writing a dozen essays that basically say the same thing.

Speak to your audience

If a particular scholarship application has requirements that indicate they are looking for a specific area of interest, cater your essay to speak to that interest. For example, if the scholarship is from, say, a foundation that supports healthcare interests, then change the area of interest in your essay to be something in healthcare, like nursing or becoming a doctor. Don't forget to change the major you detail in the essay! It is recommended not to change the school, however, because many scholarships are made out to your university, designated for you (they get a benefit on their taxes for giving to a non-profit organization). True, it's not your intended major or career path, but we're talking about money for college. You can bet that if your interest is engineering, and you are applying for a scholarship from an engineering organization, there will be other applicants competing against you that have little interest in engineering. It's unfortunate, but it's how the scholarship game is played. Go get yours.

Sometimes the odds of you getting a scholarship from a submitted application are more in your favor than you think. Sometimes it may simply be your place on a giant target and the dart happens to land on you (for some scholarship committees, this is indeed how it works. And don't knock it - some investment firms have had considerable success picking stocks using this method).

Make sure you complete the entire application. Double check every entry and make sure no blanks are left. Twice I received scholarships in college for simply being one of the few applicants who actually completed the form. It totaled over $4,000. The sole reason I was awarded both scholarships was the fact that I took the time to fill out the application form in its entirety.

Once you are certain of where you will be attending college, and you've been accepted, make a trip to the university's financial aid office and talk with their officers. There are a plethora of scholarships given by the school and its alumni for you to apply for. At least once every semester make a return trip to this office to fill out more applications and find out if there are any new or additional scholarships for which you can apply. Visit so often that they know you by name on sight. The financial aid office may know something that your school's financial aid catalog doesn't. You never know – they might receive a new scholarship endowment mid-semester and call you immediately to apply. Sometimes decisions are made based on knowledge of a student and the decision-makers impression of what kind of student they are.

You may find that one year you get a scholarship that you didn't get previously for some small, insignificant reason that has become significant now. Often it is the case that you and your family's financial situation are different than the previous year, and this may open you up for more or other scholarships.

Another place to look is into local and national non-profit organizations. Masonic Lodges, Elks, Knights of Columbus and other organizations have money that they donate to high school and college students and you don't have to be affiliated or know anyone affiliated with the group to get their financial aid.

If you belong to any recognized minority group (i.e. you are African-American, Hispanic, Asian-American, Native American, etc.) then great news! You have excellent opportunities to get financial aid because there are many scholarship foundations that exist strictly for those not in the majority. Jump on this chance if you qualify and use these organizations' generosity to your advantage and get tuition money.

Don't be afraid to go to your extended family and friends and ask their help in hunting down scholarships and other grants for college tuition. I received two scholarships that started with a conversation between my mother and her hairstylist. It never hurts to have a close network of family and friends to help you, especially when the going gets tough. And the going will get tough.

Notice that I haven't really mentioned anything about the size of scholarships as a determining factor. Never look at the size of a scholarship and say it's not worth your time. Most people don't receive those large, made-in-the-shade scholarships, but lots of people do get the smaller ones. It's better to have a little bit of something than a lot of nothing. Besides, it doesn't take much to make a bunch of smaller scholarships add up to match or exceed that lucrative big money scholarship.

Students who collect the most money in scholarships are not necessarily the smartest academically, but the ones who don't give up. They don't leave themselves with any other alternative than to apply for scholarships, and then apply for more, then more after that. To them, student loans are for those who give up the hunt for scholarships. So what are you waiting for? All you have to do is fill out the paperwork. And don't stop once you start college. There is a whole world of scholarships available only to enrolled college students, even some explicitly for undergraduate juniors, seniors, and even post- graduate funds. Basically, don't stop looking until you walk across the stage and get your diploma. Relentlessly hunt them down.

There are millions of dollars out there that are on no lists, in no financial aid office, on no rosters and generally not advertised. This money goes to those who dig it up. So dig, and dig deep.

5 OF TEXTBOOKS & TEACHERS

Of Textbooks...

Not long ago I was at my parents' farm, cleaning up various flotsam and jetsam behind their barn. As I was milling among the reeds, I stumbled across an old four-cylinder engine that I gutted for parts when I was in college. I started pulling the reeds to get closer to the engine supports. What I found supporting the block were a couple of milk crates half buried in the ground, and a small stack of books.   Upon closer examination I realized they were old textbooks from college. I could tell instantly just how much knowledge I had gotten out of the books: two books were still in a protective plastic wrapping, while a third I could tell was in the same state of disuse judging by the fact that it was an art history book.

I retrieved the books. The price tags were still on them: $70.65, $89.98, $35.76. Suddenly I was depressed. I had spent $196.39 in books and never even broke the seal! Worse yet, I had not sold them back to the bookstore or a fellow student. Now the books are too outdated to be of any value to anyone.   I cursed at the books (as if it was their fault that I lost so much money) and discreetly threw them away. I sincerely believe that is the most I've ever paid for engine stands.

The moral of the story is this:

Don't buy new books, and don't buy books you're not going to use.

You've probably heard it said dozens of times from dozens of different people that it is cheaper to buy used books. Of course! It certainly doesn't take a genius to figure out that used books are going to save you money. They contain pages, pictures and information identical to a new book at a fraction of the cost. You can save hundreds over the course of your college career, and make out just as well as the Senator's son who's too good to buy used.

Used textbooks are not only cheaper, but for some of us there might be an added advantage. Some used books will have markings left by other students who have taken the class, or better yet, the professor, before. Sometimes the markings are random scribbling or stupid remarks like "Biology 101 sucks. Word up" or "North State Football Rules!" which offer no help in your pursuit of knowledge (except that this may be a sign that the class or the professor is a real bore). However, other times the markings might contain valuable information, some interesting insight written off to the side that you can mention in class or on the test and appear to be the genius that you are. You might find the main points or, better yet, test questions and answers highlighted on key pages. If you like someone else taking notes for you, this might be a great tool to have. But certainly this is not for everyone. Many people would rather put the notes in themselves - that way they know that everything in the book is theirs, not someone else's. It is your choice to make, but do be aware that some of the used books may contain writing inside, so you may choose to use this to your advantage or look for a textbook that's void of notes and highlights.

You don't have to buy textbooks at the campus bookstore.

The campus bookstore normally carries both new and used textbooks, but often they are the highest cost books on the market. You are essentially paying a premium for the convenience of having them readily available. They charge these high prices because they have an almost captive buying audience. They also charge them because their target customer base is a small community of students, not a large metropolis of multiple groups with multiple interests and more discretionary spending. These truths do not come to mind when standing in line looking at a $400 purchase of textbooks. What does come to mind I cannot mention here without attaching a parental advisory label. And that means you have to involve legal, and who wants that?

You may also look to other places for the same book. Online outlets, off-campus bookstores and campus message boards are loaded with less costly alternatives. Several websites exist today that allow you to rent the book for a fraction of the cost of purchasing. This can be a valid alternative for those core classes that you have to take but, once complete, will move on without needing to reference it in the future (I'm looking at you, Speech 101). Some examples of places to source textbooks:

www.half.com (to purchase)

www.chegg.com (to rent)

Check out the message boards around campus, especially at the beginning and end of each semester as students who don't want to take such a hit selling their books back to the bookstore will place flyers around campus advertising their books on sale. Make sure it is the right book you are looking for, and try negotiating a lower price than what they are asking for it. You can really come out ahead.

For those a little more comfortable with risk, there is an even more effective way to save money on textbooks:

Don't buy or rent the textbook until you have to.

Just because the book is listed on your syllabus does not necessarily mean that your professor will ever crack it open or ask you to do so. Most professors test off of their notes, and the textbook is just something that the school requires them to have, or as suggested additional reading. Some teachers have never even read the book that they are saying you must have for the class! If you can get by without the book, why buy it?

Of course you don't know if you need the book until you've started the course and get a feel for the professor and his or her teaching methods. If a professor assigns reading, then by all means buy or rent the book ASAP, because there may be something in there that you will need to know. True, you might not be able to find the textbook at that time at the bookstore, and might need to spend extra money online having a book shipped overnight, but I have found that when comparing the costs of buying every textbook to renting every textbook to avoiding any textbook expense unless absolutely necessary, the avoiding strategy is hands down the most cost efficient way.

When you do have to purchase a book, consider putting it up for sale around campus or online. I've had more than one experience where I sold a textbook for more than I paid for it by purchasing online at a deep discount and then offering it around campus at slightly less than the bookstore's price. Imagine getting paid to have that textbook!

This is not to say never buy a textbook. If the course is part of your major and you think you might use it as a reference after you're out of school and in the "real world," then get the book. And naturally if you are just very interested in the subject and enjoy the reading when it is not required, then it is perfectly alright to spend the money.

This suggestion to avoid purchasing a textbook is mainly for those core courses that you are required to take but know that you will never make use of the book. Let's face it - there are required courses that do not pertain to your major or your interests that universities require in order to "round out" your education. Don't get me wrong, it is good to expand your mind, but if you can do that without expanding your overall debt, then do it. You might also employ this money-saving method for courses that you think you might drop, like electives that turn out to be more damaging to your GPA than help. This way, when you drop the class after six weeks you don't have to go back to the bookstore and find out that the book that you got no use of is now valued at 35% of what you paid for it.

Use this same approach when it comes to graphing calculators, lab supplies, and any other sundries you may need for class. Waiting until you need it may save you money when you actually don't need it at all.

...& Teachers.

I'm going to ruin university for some of you with this story, but I think it should be told to remind us of the big picture. I was talking to a veterinarian right before I went to college and he told me something very interesting about his college experience. He went to the school of veterinary medicine at a particular university on a lot of academic scholarships because he did so well in high school. At the veterinary school he studied hard, made excellent grades, and was always the head of the class, yada, yada, yada. You know the type. Finally he fulfilled all of the required courses to graduate with his veterinary degree. At the graduation, the school walked the graduates across the stage to get their diplomas just like any other school, with one exception - the graduates did not walk across in alphabetical order. Rather, they walked across in order of their GPA. You see, the school decided to conduct a social experiment – they informed all the veterinary school students, on their first day of their first course, that upon graduation they would walk across the stage in order of their GPA rather than their last name. The idea was to see if it motivated the class to outperform previous classes in terms of studies and scholastic performance. The school attempted where possible to repeat past curriculums to maintain other factors in the experiment as much as possible.

So my veterinary friend, being the good student that he was, walked across the stage fairly early in the list; not first, but high enough to be proud of himself and his accomplishments. The last person to walk across the stage had the worst GPA of all the graduating class. This meant that he was the worst student. And this also meant that everyone else knew he was the worst student. What he must have thought of himself that day, being dead last among his peers, I perish to think. My friend then explained that at this school, there was a special term used for this last person to cross the stage - it was "doctor."

I do not tell you this to discourage you from doing your best, nor am I giving you an excuse to be lazy and do the minimum required. I tell you this to explain that in most circumstances it is not the end of the world if you do not make straight A's. Sometimes it's better to have a B and devote more time and energy to earning tuition money, or digging deeper to learn a particular piece of knowledge, than graduating Summa Cum Laude with a $50,000 school bill. Chances are very slim that your future employer will ever see your college transcripts. And most employers don't really care; they just want to see that you have at least a foundational knowledge of a subject upon which they can build, and that you showed that you can commit several years to a single goal and accomplish what you set out to do.

As with so many things, there are exceptions to this axiom. If you are planning on pursuing a career in academia, or pushing for medical school, or any other higher degree beyond the undergraduate level, or even if you think you might one day pursue a higher degree beyond the undergraduate level, then put the effort into making the best grades that you can. You might not discover that one extra $500 scholarship, but if it means getting into a better school for your post-secondary education, then it is worth the financial sacrifice. In truth, those people that are committed to controlling the cost of their education are often also committed to getting the best grades. These students always find a way to do both.

So with this, let's explore a few more areas that can guide you smoothly through college:

Take the professor - not the course.

Before you sign up for classes, start asking around and find out who the best teachers are, who the easiest teachers are, and who the hardest teachers are. Depending on your degree plan, and where you want your college education to carry you, start planning ahead with each semester and school year and keep track of which professors you want to avoid and which ones you want to sign up with whenever possible. And this will vary with your situation as there really is no one-size-fits-all program I can offer you. Just know that, before you start picking classes, you may want to consider this:

If you are signing up for a core course, and you know you are generally not interested in the subject but have to have it as part of your degree, find the easiest professor you can. The last thing you want is a calculus course hurting the GPA of your pre-law endeavor. As a Biology major, don't kill yourself studying for a ridiculously hard Survey of World History quiz if you've got an anatomy test coming up. You've got much bigger fish to fry…or possibly dissect.

If you really enjoy being challenged, and perform better when you are under more pressure, then find out who the hardest professors are and take them, knowing that the extra burden will push you to work harder and do better. Know thyself.

For those courses that are required by your major field of study, I would recommend that you find out who the best professors are; the ones who will give you the most information that you will use when you join the working masses. These instructors might be hard or easy as far as making the grade is concerned, but the knowledge that they will empower you with is going to be priceless. I knew many students who took the higher road with a harder class because they knew they would get in return information that no textbook or course guide can teach.

There is an exception for those seeking academic careers after graduating – in academia, it matters who you learned under, so seek out those professors that have the most notoriety to enhance your chances of future academic success.

Sometimes you will find that the best professor might also be the easiest, or conversely the hardest professor might be the one that will give you the most knowledge for your buck. I had a professor once who was the easiest as well as the best. And yet, he was also the hardest. The reason? In my small private university, he was the only professor who taught the course. You just have to weigh your options and balance your course load with the best teachers for your major and the easiest ones for your core courses. Unless, of course, you like a real challenge. Or you're a masochist.

I also suggest that, if you plan to work "in the real world" after you graduate, then seek out those professors teaching your major who spent a significant portion of their professional past practicing in the field in which they profess. These practitioners will teach you more practical knowledge over the duration of the course, and more of that information will translate to the job once you have it.

As an example, an academic professor will teach you how to calculate the Weighted Average Cost of Capital (WACC), because it is important for research, publications and other academic pursuits. A professor who used it in real capital markets will tell you where you go to get the current WACC for a particular sector, and how it is used in decision-making. For me, the latter is worth its weight in gold. For the future PhD student next to me, the former has the shiniest luster.

Naturally, as an incoming freshman, you will find it more difficult to determine which teachers to take. Many of us spend the first semester or freshman year getting our bearing on which route to take as far as teachers go. We suffer because we do not know who to turn to with these questions (some of us don't even know to ask these questions - that's why this book is being written). Feel free to ask your academic advisor. This is the professor you are assigned to who guides you through the process of which classes to sign up for, and what order you should take some of the classes, especially with regards to your major. Be honest with them, and most likely they will be up front with you. Also, if you will be residing in a dorm, ask your resident advisor. If you'll be playing sports, definitely ask your coaches, as they are enthusiastically interested in you getting by with the easiest core classes the school has to offer. By the end of your freshman year, you will have a group of friends and fellow students who will have either been there, done that, or knew someone who has. So get the low down on whom to take, and make your class load much more efficient so that you can get the most out of what is important to you without losing so many sleepless nights over something of less consequence.

Make friends with your professors.

When I was in high school I tried out for the JV baseball team. Not to blow my own trumpet, but I was a decent first baseman. I knocked a few balls out of the park during the tryouts, made only two errors in the field, and generally did a good job fitting in with the team. The head coach had a son who also played baseball. He was not the most gifted player - he struggled sometimes hitting the ball, made more than a few errors in the field, and easily was the slowest runner (I was not the fastest runner myself, but I always knew I wouldn't finish last as long as he was on the field). When time came to cut those players they didn't want, I was on that list. I was not surprised, as this was Texas, where Friday night football is king. Why would they cut a football player and risk losing him in the Fall for a baseball player they know isn't going to play football? However, the slowest runner on the team made the cut. Why? When was the last time a coach ever cut his own son from a sports team?

A professor is less likely to fail you if he or she has a vested interest in you. So how do you get them interested in you? The first week walk up to them immediately after class and ask them a quick question about what was discussed in class. This shows them that you are interested in learning the material, and they will put a face to a name. Repeat often throughout the semester to reinforce in their mind your existence and interest in the course. Often in major universities there are so many students in any given class that students simply become numbers to the professors. But if they remember that Johnny Q. has asked him or her a few questions outside of class, has participated in class, and has taken an interest in the material, he or she will likely give you some slack if there is a questionable answer given on a test. Some professors will outright give you an A! Most of the time if you know you are close to making a higher grade you can ask the professor for some extra credit and he or she might extend you this chance to raise your score. They would not be as likely if they did not know you from the next student in class. So make friends with your professors. Seek them out after class, and periodically schedule conferences with them to go over your grades and course material. Sit at the front of the class to remind them you are there. Plus it scores some major brownie points because it looks like you're even more interested than you may actually be.

Carry a reasonable course load.

The average full-time college student takes somewhere between 13 - 15 hours each semester, or about 5 classes. For those new to the "hours" terminology, the term refers to how many hours you will be in class each week for a semester. You will have to determine what is a reasonable course load for you, but generally following the average is your best bet for getting your degree without wasting extra years in school, or working yourself to death trying to graduate so that you can get out there and.....well.....work yourself to death. I would recommend taking a light course load your first semester (say, four classes), as you are still adjusting to a new environment. Many of us find ourselves living on our own for the first time in our lives, and for some this is hard to get adjusted to. Also, for those of us from smaller communities there is a culture shock of being suddenly surrounded by so many people with different viewpoints, many of whom will try and influence young and impressionable minds. Four classes would be a reasonable course load for your first semester. You can always take extra classes down the line, after you've made a complete adjustment to college life and are comfortable with your academic achievements, what you can do while balancing work and social activities. Be sure that the courses you take fall in line with the requirements of your particular degree program.

Electives should be a no-brainer.

Electives are just as the name implies - something you don't have to take, but elect to take because you are interested in the subject. So why would you choose to take Advanced Thermodynamics if you are a Speech Communications major? Don't make your course load harder than it has to be.

I had a friend at school who wanted to take a very special class. Let's call her Micah. This class was offered only in spring of odd years, and by the time Micah met the prerequisites for the class she had only one chance to take it. It was an elective for her major field of study, and the class really interested her. So she signed up for it, and the class proved to be very interesting. It also proved to be one of the hardest classes she was taking in a semester that also consisted of Physics II (with lab), Greek IV and Interdisciplinary Philosophy. Micah knew that this would be the only chance she would have to take this class, but there were so many outside assignments for each class that it was going to be quite a struggle to do well in this class as well as her other, required courses. Micah realistically assessed that her GPA would suffer, and as she would pursue higher level degrees, she knew she had to watch her GPA. As much as she would have enjoyed taking the elective, she dropped it and picked up something much easier so that she could focus more attention on the required courses and an elective that would take care of itself with minimal input. It was quite a sacrifice, but now that Micah is out of school she has found time to read all about the subject that she was so interested in.

Non-major electives should be no-brainers. They should be easy A's that require little to no stress on you so that more time and energy can be focused on those courses that matter most. They will help boost your GPA if you are pursuing post-grad education, and could make an otherwise dismal report card look brighter when your parents ask how you did last semester.

Take all of this into consideration whenever you are mapping out your degree path. Remember - try to buy cheaper books that are used, and if at all possible, do not buy them at all. Take the professor - not the class, so that you can increase your opportunities for a higher GPA. And manage your course load whenever you can, so you can focus more of your attention and study time to the classes that matter most. It certainly beats being broke around mid-terms and no chance for finding work because you don't have the time away from your books to get a job.

6 MONEY

Money. Moolah. Cold, hard cash. Greenbacks. Dough. Bread. Gs and Ks. We've got a thousand names for it, and we could probably use a thousand right now to pay those college application fees. While it is worshipped by some and eschewed by others, the fact remains, money buys options. The more money you have, the more options you have. And for most students preparing for college, money is a very scarce resource.

There are legions of books dedicated to managing your money. This book will not go into nearly the detail that those books do, but it will provide some general guidelines, all basically summed up by what was discussed in the first chapter – live on less money than you make.

Thankfully, in college you will find yourself surrounded by other students who feel just as cash-poor as you do. It becomes quite acceptable to be stingy with small purchases, taking free handouts and advantages of student discounts and other beneficial pricing when available. It almost becomes a badge of honor. You will find yourself eating ramen noodles, canned green beans and counting down the days to 60 cent Taco Tuesdays more times than you will care to admit. Socially, it's very acceptable not to have the latest fashions in the closet or newest car in the parking lot.

You will find your friends bragging about how they accomplished some life hack instead of paying the full cost of something. You'll find yourself doing the same. Adjusting that pizza coupon with Photoshop to get another $2 knocked off the price? Been there. Rented space on a couch for a month rather than pay rent? Definitely done that. We do what we have to do in order to get by. It can even carry over after you graduate. I'm 42 and even today, when I go to the movies, I instinctively mention that I have my student ID and show it to them to see if they will knock a couple of dollars of the price of a ticket.

One thing you should really be wary of is credit cards. With your bank account and new mailing address, many credit card companies will undoubtedly send you all kinds of offers in the mail, promising you "purchasing power" and "easy payments." The reason they are hitting up a college student who very likely does not have the money to pay the average credit card bill? Because the industry knows that statistically you are more likely to hold onto that very first credit card far longer than any other, even if it is a higher interest rate or has the least favorable terms. Credit card companies are in a race to reach you first.

Credit cards are a subject that you should discuss at length with your parents. They no doubt have experience in this area, and can advise you with whether or not credit cards are right for you, and if so, which ones.

It is strongly advised to limit the exposure to, and use of credit cards. There should be nothing that you need to purchase right now for which you have no money. If you cannot afford to buy something with cash, then ask yourself if you truly need it. If it is a matter of a large purchase, consider discussing with your parents first (hint: they might even buy it for you). A second opinion can help in making the right financial decision.

Your parents may insist on you having a credit card for "emergencies." That's fine. Respect their decision and use it only in emergencies. Just make sure that a 2 a.m. cheeseburger craving does not constitute an emergency. And if you do choose to get a credit card, don't take it with you around town. Leave it in your sock drawer or change jar where it's not easily available when Jay-Z's next album drops. Be very wary of credit cards. They can be a helpful asset in building a credit history, but if improperly managed, they can be a ruthless master over you. As a comedian once mused, "whoever came up with the idea of 'easy payments' has never had to pay it." There's no such thing as an easy payment.

Without a doubt the biggest purchase you may have is a vehicle. This one area can make or break your chances of paying off college and graduating without owing any money to the school. Some will find it easier than others if their parents still have their old Toyota Tercel sitting behind the garage. But for those of you who do not have this luxury, purchasing a vehicle is a very big deal, and one in which you should consult extensively with both your parents and every other adult you know before you put dollar one into any motorized transportation. And this is a place where you will definitely need to leave your pride at the doorstep.

I'll tell you a story about a high school friend and myself. We'll call him Mark. We both got trucks when we turned 16, which was around the same time. They were both, ironically, the same vehicle - a 1977 Ford F-150 (in Texas, you have to own a truck or they'll kick you out of the state). Both were a very ugly brown. I can brag a little because I had a bigger engine and tan stripes. But still, how can a brown truck look cool, even with racy stripes? And with a bigger engine came more trips to the gas station. Neither one of us really liked the color of our trucks. Both of us wanted a change.

Here is where the story gets good. Mark took his truck to the shop, and painted it the second most beautiful deep black I had ever seen. Then he put some really nice wheels on with wide tires - gorgeous! Then he put a 'glass pack muffler on to make it sound loud (which also meant he couldn't exactly sneak quietly home after curfew). Finally, he had a very nice stereo system installed. It was all around an absolutely magnificent truck. In all, it cost him around $4,000 to turn his beast into a beauty.

I went a different route. I bought a brand new engine and parts straight from Ford. My father and I installed it together - a memory that we still cherish together. Everything under the hood was replaced and the transmission was rebuilt. Basically, I had a brand new vehicle underneath an old body. And it costs me around $4,000 - just like Mark.

After four months Mark had to sell his truck (ironically for $4,000 - what he paid for the upgrades) because the old engine was leaking oil and guzzling too much gas, and the transmission was starting to fail. With my new engine, I was getting better gas mileage than when the truck was new! It cranked and ran like a brand new car - it just looked ugly on the outside. While Mark lost the money that he paid for his truck, and ultimately had to buy another vehicle, I took my dependable truck off to college, where I went to school, and work, without dreading a car payment every month. In fact, I still drive it today. I could have painted the truck when I was in high school, and driven something a little cooler than "shitty brown," but then I wouldn't have graduated college debt free. It was a sacrifice that I made when I was younger so that I could live better when I was older.

If you are in a position where you don't have the family's old Toyota parked behind the garage, then consider not owning a car while you are in school. It is a luxury for most of us (indeed, it was a luxury for me - I lived within walking distance from high school as well as college, and my family had a vehicle that I could borrow for work, dates, etc.). Additionally, keep in mind that you will have to have the vehicle insured (some states require it, but it's still a good idea to have it even if your state does not). Liability insurance - the cheapest insurance – is still often expensive for young people, depending on the vehicle and your driving record. So without a vehicle, you can seriously pocket some major change for college.

If you truly have to own a vehicle while you are in school, ask your parents if any relatives have an old car or truck sitting in some barn or field that could run at least just enough to get you to school and back. Whatever you do, do not buy a brand new vehicle. Buy used, and only if you have to. The old family station wagon may not get you a date with the prom queen, but how rewarding would your relationship be dating a person who judges you by what you drive? But again, do you really need a car? Is there a bus route near you? Do you have a bike? Do you have friends who have cars? Do you have tennis shoes?

Limiting expenses should become the mantra of your college life. Whatever the situation, always be thinking if there is a way to do it for free or at very little cost. Please understand this is not to say that you should break the law or sacrifice your health in order to save a few dollars. This is to say that, with every discretionary purchase decision, consider the alternatives and go after the more cost-efficient solution. That might mean asking for a ride with friends when you go camping for the weekend, rather than driving your own car (do offer to pay for a tank of gas). It might mean getting groceries and learning to cook, rather than eating out every meal. It might mean learning to do that small repair yourself rather than taking it to a professional. Whatever the situation, always be thinking if there is a less costly way to do it.

As you get older and gain more experience, you will learn where not to cut expenses. Good attorneys, financial advisors, mechanics and doctors are among a short list of professionals where getting the best you can afford will pay off in the end. But as a college student, you shouldn't need these people or their services, because you have no assets to be sued over, you have no money, you didn't bring a car to college and you're in great health. So save your money and spend it on getting the best education.

7   STUDYING, CRAMMING & OTHER BORING STUFF

Each of us has a different way of studying, so to propose to you a one-stop solution on taking the best notes or the best way to study would be wrong. All we can say here is to know yourself, and how you listen and understand the best, and how you take notes the best, and how you study the best, and follow those tactics in college.

The same with cramming – while it is considered a taboo subject in college (at least among professors) it must be recognized that for some, it is the best way to study. The pressure of time makes us focus, and that focus helps us to remember. If that works best for you, then use it. Most students will find in college that cramming alone will not help on exams. Rather, regular studying followed by last moment cramming (that's called reviewing at that point) seems to work best for the majority of students. Know thyself.

Previously the practical concept of "taking the teacher, not the course" was discussed. Academic strategy versus real-life strategy of professors was covered. School name recognition was touched on. Now let's cover some of the other aspects of the college experience that will help you gain knowledge, experience, and possibly set yourself up for a very successful career. It's the Other Boring Stuff of the chapter (spoiler alert: it's not that boring).

Get a mentor.

Meeting regularly with someone who has more experience than you can pay huge dividends in your own educational richness and personal maturity. They can guide you on which classes to take, which professors to take, what the job market looks like and what it is forecasted to look like, and so on. Many times they will help you find your first job. It is strongly advised that throughout your life, seek mentors. And somewhere along the way, be a mentor. You enrich your life as much giving as you do receiving.

Get involved.

Make it a point to get involved in student-based organizations. They will do well to enrich your education experience, and at little to no cost to you. On campuses across every university in America, you will find countless fraternities, sororities, social groups, clubs, religious organizations and societies to provide interaction with other students, professors, school staff and supporters – all people who can become something of a family away from family. They can enhance your studies, such as joining a finance club while you're taking finance courses. Student organizations often have mentor programs to pair you with a mentor, making it easier to find someone who can guide you on your college journey.

Organizations can expand your awareness of social and cultural issues. Many students raised in one culture or religion might find value in joining a student organization of another culture or religion, just to become more aware of the differences (and more often than not, the similarities) that make up this planet's cultural fabric. Some student organizations keep questions and keys to some professor's exams!

Study abroad.

At the Masters level, one area where a financial cost that could be saved might be well spent is in a solid Study Abroad program. I propose to you that no good Master's program is worth its salt without a great Study Abroad program.

Under these programs, you spend an amount of time (2 weeks to a full semester) in another country, often with fellow students, doing work and

COLLEGE ON A DIME

learning in a different environment. It is an expense that you can live without, but you will be missing a very big component of your education experience. The cultural exchange is certainly enriching, but it also helps you to see situations and problems from different viewpoints. It helps you look at your own country from a different viewpoint. You find yourself more knowledgeable of the world (read: many Americans tend to be unaware of world events) and how it impacts this country. You might even find a career there after you graduate. You will find a great time. And you will build unforgettable memories. After all, life begins at the edge of your comfort zone. And above all, Study Abroad programs are great ways to build a solid core network of people.

Build your network.

Mentors, student orgs, fraternities, study abroad – all of these recommendations are to accomplish something very specific. They help to build your network of friends, business contacts and other connections. As you approach college graduation, you will be starting your career, and it is this network of people that you have built up over the years that you can reach out to in order to land those first jobs. Thus, the larger your networks, the better the odds of getting help from your connections. It's just how the world works. I keep the advice from a fortune cookie taped to my wallet. It reads:

A wise person knows everything. A shrewd person – everyone.

Knowing lots of people from different backgrounds, interests, careers and so on can become a critical tool in landing the right job to get your career started, saving you from costly mistakes, keeping your actions in line with your morals, or simply a great group of people to enjoy spending time with.

8   WORK, WORK, WORK

Jane was a real go-getter. For most of her college life, she worked at a restaurant on campus. Starting out washing dishes, she showed her hard work ethic, which got the attention of the restaurant managers. So she was promoted, first to food prep, then to sous-chef, and finally to restaurant manager. Each time, Jane was given a higher wage, along with more responsibility.

It was hard work, and certainly more effort, both mentally and physically than when she started out washing dishes. But it was also more pay. She was earning more dollars for the same hour of labor. Thus, she was putting more dollars in the bank. And at the end of each shift, Jane would go right back to her apartment and dive into her course notes. She was on a mission. Her mission was to graduate.

The more you work, the more you earn, and the less time you have to

spend it.

While there is something to be said about enjoying the college experience (more on that in the next chapter) there's also something to be said about working during college. Working helps you prioritize your time. Because so much of it is filled with earning income (as small as it might seem), you have to maximize the remaining time for school, for sleep, and for the best fun that you can have with what time is left. And because so much of that time is filled with activities that do not involve spending money, there is less time left for you to spend that cash. Thus, you save more.

This book is not going to suggest that you work 40 hours a week while going for that engineering degree. Nor is it going to sugarcoat and say that you can get by working two hours a week. You know your ability, and the amount of time that you need to study and make good grades. This book suggests that you do work some amount each week while you are in school. Working what you can will help you maximize your income while minimizing your expenses, not to mention maximizing your time.

Consider working part time during the semester. Find a very easy job that offers you flexibility, and most importantly understands that your priority is to get a college degree. The best employers will recognize your priorities, and do their best to flex around you. Usually, in return they get a hard worker that is loyal, and that does not cost them as much money. Translation: you might not make that much money per hour working for them, but you will be able to work for them.

Where you can really maximize your income is during the summer months as well as the winter break. During these stretches of time, if you are not in class, try to be earning money. There are many summer jobs that are typical for college students, like summer camp counsellorships, retail stores, amusement parks, lifeguarding posts and the like, all looking for extra help to handle increased demand during the summer months. I am a particular fan of any summer job where you can stay for free, eat for free, play for free, and earn money in the meantime. That could mean summer camp, but it can also mean staying with your parents, or grabbing a friend's couch while you work full-time.

The winter break, as well as Spring Break, offer opportunities to maximize the time that you have to earn an income and minimize expenses. The Christmas shopping season always has a demand for retail employees, so look to your nearest retail outlets for a nice little bump in hours (and, thus, pay) after you have finished your semester exams. Ditto Spring Break. Accounting firms, river rafting outfits, bars and party venues all need extra staff during this time. Yes, you might run into some of your classmates and friends while working security at the Red Hot Chili Peppers concert, but you also might find yourself having a drink with Flea!

Flexibility is the name of the game when working during the semester. Your priority is education, so any work that you do needs to be able to flex around your schedule. Let's face it, exams, papers and projects all rise and fall in demand over the course of the semester, so the demands for your attention rise and fall concordantly. So any work that you can do that can flex around that is great. Drive for Uber, be a freelance writer or secret shopper. Do a fashion blog.

One place to consider is sales. It is not really glamorous, and it is not for everybody, but it will definitely teach you a lot in the process. Participating in a sales program, even on a small scale can teach you a lot. You will learn what tactics work, and which ones don't, and what you would do if you were to do it full-time. Often sales positions can allow you to be flexible with your hours and your energy. But most importantly, if you pursue it honestly, you will walk away with a skill set that you can use in any position in your future career. After all, what are you doing in a job interview? Selling your skills.

In any of your work situations, if you find yourself working in an environment that is not conducive to your educational success, leave immediately. These are bad bosses or fellow employees, dangerous work environments, companies that promote unethical behavior, or anything that intervenes in your education. You can always find another position somewhere else. It is not worth your time to endure barriers to your success.

For this reason, I would suggest looking into work-study programs. These are programs whereby you are employed by the University, usually as a professor's assistant or other doer of small tasks. Often you are required to commit to a set number of hours in a given week, but the school, knowing the need for your schedule to be flexible, will offer you the flexibility with your hours. And more times than not, you will spend some of those hours with nothing to do, so you study! Imagine being paid to study for your next exam. Awesome concept!

Being a resident advisor is also an opportunity for you to get paid to study. The resident advisor is a student that lives in the dorms, usually for free or greatly reduced cost. They often enjoy free or reduced cost meal programs as well. Their task is often nothing more than being a listening ear for other students, making sure that nobody gets too rowdy or loud in the dorms, and being a student voice for those living on campus. Easy job, easy money, and flexibility for your study needs. Perfect. One of the resident advisors in my dorm also worked part-time near the campus, so he was effectively living for free, eating for free, getting a stipend for living expenses from the university, and earning income working at the nearby business. For a college student, he was rolling in it!

9 PLAY, PLAY, PLAY

There we were, backstage, just me and my mates, and a few guys from a little group called Depeche Mode, discussing how they used synthesizers in the early 80s when the technology was truly in its infancy (good idea), and taking shots of tequila (bad idea).

For much of my time as an undergraduate, I managed a little rock band. We had some moderate success – toured Europe, Asia, and got to meet and open for some truly remarkable acts, often times before they were household names. Importantly, we were able to perform for a number of years and make a little money in the process. For me it was an opportunity to take a small gamble at making a considerable sum of money while being around great music – something that I loved dearly. It was also an excuse to get out of town on weekends.

One year we were able to score some free tickets to see Depeche Mode in concert (how I got the tickets is another story, not fit for print). They were a big influence on the guys in the band. The concert was amazing. One of the opening singers – Poe – absolutely stunned the crowd with her performance.

During the opening acts, Jimmy, who simultaneously plays bass guitar and has no limit to his comfort zone, noticed what to any musician would be obvious – one of the backstage entrances. So he grabs us and we wedge our way through the crowd, around the side of the stage, and squarely up to the biggest bouncer I have ever seen in my life. He was a wall. Jimmy says "hey. Is Depeche Mode back there?" To which the bouncer casually replied, "Maybe." That was Jimmy's invitation to make a new friend.

Jimmy: "How do we get back there?"

The Wall: "You gotta have tickets"

Jimmy pulls out a $20 bill…

Jimmy: Does the ticket look anything like this?

The Wall: It looks a lot like that.

The bouncer grabbed the Jackson, stepped aside (which kind of resembled the blast door at NORAD opening to make way) and the five of us rushed through before he had a chance to clarify if the twenty was for all, or he expected one from each of us. The rest is history.

Twenty bucks to hang backstage with Depeche Mode, talk shop and do tequila shots! Best. Concert. Ever.

Carpe diem, baby.

One of the outright joys of college life is the combination of youth, freedom and minimal responsibility. So while much of this book is dedicated to getting a college education on as little expense as possible, it is important to note that if taken to the extreme, you may find yourself regretting that you didn't take advantage of at least some of the thrills of being young and free. Enjoy your college days, build those relationships, make those occasional late night pizza runs, and build those memories. They will stay with you forever.

Taking out extra money on your student loan to spend Spring Break in Cabo might not be the best way to build memories. That debt may linger almost as long as your memories and you might find yourself regretting the trip because the cost was so dear. Look for free or low cost adventures to go on. You can build the same incredible memories without the high overhead. And remember, whatever your financial situation, and at any moment, there is always Ultimate Frisbee on the Quad.

Some other suggestions:

1) Movie rentals. Grab your BFFs, pool your pocket change together and rent a movie. Or three. Have a popcorn-infused rom-com marathon in the Student Center. Pick a theme for the night and choose your movies accordingly. Worst acting ever, best B-movies, CryFest – whatever marathon you want to run, it will cost pennies, and bring you and your friends closer together.
2) The great outdoors. Grab some friends and head to a state park or recreational area to get some fresh air, exercise and stories around the campfire. The cost is minimal and you can build treasured memories. Just don't forget the s'mores.
3) Café culture. Relax over a latte and solve the world's problems with your friends, or even a few strangers. Revolutions have started over late night cups of java – start your own.
4) Learn an instrument. Learn to code. Blast storm troopers. If you want some quality time alone, find low cost ways to enjoy the solitude. Find a quiet place to meditate, or teach yourself to paint. There are endless possibilities for the introvert in all of us.
5) Explore. Go for a drive, and explore the city around you. Take a road you've never driven before. It only costs a little gas. And if you bike, it costs you nothing.
6) Hit the gym. Head to the rec center, alone or with a posse. Everyone will feel good, and if your gym has a sauna, you can relax for a good hour, laughing, chatting and sweating your ass off. As good as a massage, only free (well, technically included in the semester's fees). It's great fun.
7) Hang out with the prof. Many professors are in academia partly because they are invigorated by being surrounded by young people, with their enthusiasm and ideals. This carries over outside of class as well, so as you spend time with your course instructors, you might find yourself having dinner (can you say free home-cooked meal?) at their house with friends, or hanging out at the blues bar and talking about that time you stood in line with Gatemouth Brown to buy tickets to see Eric Clapton. You might even find yourself learning a few inside tips on other professors, their courses, and how to get the most of the class.
8) Go fly a kite. Grab a Frisbee, football, soccer ball or just a journal and head to the park. You'll get fresh air, sunshine, and possibly a new perspective on a class problem simply by the change of surroundings.

9) Cook. If you have a kitchen (or access to one), pitch in some change, grab a bag of groceries and spend a few hours cooking with friends. The longer the cooking time, the better. This is especially good with international students, who can bring authentic provincial recipes to your table of six for less than the cost of a deep dish pepperoni.

10) Get creative. There are myriad ways to have fun for free in college. Have a grocery budget? See if you can best last week's grocery expenses with a lower food bill. Plan your restaurant visits to coincide with all the Taco Tuesdays, Friday Flapjacks and Super Saver Sundays. Bike to work and class. Sell your old toys and childhood detritus online as "collectors' items." Audit courses that you are interested in. There are so many things you can do for fun. Be imaginative.

These were 10 things that my friends and I came up with in three minutes. Imagine what kind of interesting (epic!) memories you can create with a little ingenuity and a commitment to not touch the pocketbook. Perhaps the best things in life really are free.

10 POST GRADUATE OVER-EDUCATED OUT OF WORK BLUES

Musician Wally Pleasant summed it up well when he wrote the song Post Graduate Over-Educated Out-of-Work Blues. It is a lovely little lament about graduating college without a job, and unfortunately it is a very common experience among many graduating students. The National Center for Education Statistics reported in 2015 that among 20-24 year olds in the US, 51% with less than a high school diploma were employed, whereas 89% of college graduates had some form of employment – a solid argument for getting a college degree. Still, that's an 11% unemployment rate for students in this age range with a degree. And it is not factoring in the quality of work for that student with a Bachelor or higher. Translation: it might be difficult to get a position after you graduate, and it will be more difficult to get a position in the field of your interest.

That's why it is important to be working on a job long before you walk across that stage for your diploma. The effort you put into your search for a position once you graduate will have a huge determination on your future trajectory. While some land feet first into plush positions at great companies, most of us have to slog it out and get that first job through sheer grit and determination. And the sooner you get started on this, the better.

Network.

Remember that word from earlier? Here it is again, because it's when you're hunting for work that it really makes a difference. It is usually at this point that many students realize that, while they may know everything about nuclear physics, they know no one who is a nuclear physicist, or who works in that area.

Leverage your network by reaching out to them, continuing to cultivate your relationships, to see who they know or what they have heard about work, companies, people they know, etc. Technology solutions such as LinkedIn have made it far easier to "technically" network with others, exchange contact information, research names and history on people, but nothing beats sitting across the table from one of your friends, bonding over a cup of coffee and a shared memory, and discussing who they know that might lead you to a position.

Who do your parents know? They already have a lifelong network built up that they should be able to reach out to in order to help you find work. Use their connections (in the most respectful way, because you are effectively leasing someone else's network) if it is available.

Remember those mentors you met with monthly all those years of school? Who do they know? Do they know what your interests are and where you would like to work? They have a network of friends and family that you can borrow as well. Again, be respectful of their contacts and walk through each point of contact you want to make with their network, what you are going to say, and the details.

Networking goes both ways.

Networking is a two way street. To get, you need to give as well. Always be looking to help others in their own searching, because it will generate goodwill towards you and might open the door for a position at another time. If all you do is take from others without giving, do you expect them to keep giving forever? You don't need me to tell you this – your parents have been telling you this your entire life.

Have your elevator pitch ready.

Letting people know that you are looking for a job is one thing. But if you cannot clarify what specifically you want to do with your career, then it will be very difficult for anyone to help you. That's why it is important to have a small "elevator pitch" prepared for you to draw on whenever the opportunity arises. An elevator pitch, if you are unfamiliar with the term, is a brief synopsis of what you are selling (in this case, you). It must be short, to the point, and at the same time intriguing enough to warrant further discussion. The term comes from the scenario where a salesperson gets on the same elevator as the CEO or other decision-maker of a company. The salesperson has only as long as the elevators ride to "pitch" the product or service they are selling. You must have the same kind of pitch ready for those random moments when the opportunity arises to let someone know you are looking for career opportunities. So have a brief, 2-3 sentence speech that you can draw upon in those random circumstances where you meet someone in public, after a presentation, at a company visit, or wherever, when you have a very short time to make a big impression on someone who might become your employer.

Make Career Services work for you.

Almost every university has a career services department. They might go by a different name, and not be well known across campus, but their sole responsibility as a group is to help locate employment for their students. Get to know these people. They will have their ear to what the markets are demanding, and can help you not only find open positions, but can help you craft your resume, prepare for your interview, and give you some inside tips on the organization. Make friends with them. Bake them cookies. Offer to help out in the Career Services Center. Do whatever you can to be at the top of their mind when a new position is sent to the department for fulfillment. They are a great resource for open positions, internships, development programs and other employment options.

Prod the prof.

Professors are also great resources for job hunting. Remember that professor that befriended you, had you and your friends over for dinner, and discussed which professors you should take? They might also have a suggestion of which employers to reach out to. And they might even make an introduction for you. Remember that professor in whose class you sat at the back, never asked a question, never spoke to after class and never did anything beyond the minimum required effort to complete the course? Of course you don't remember the professor. They don't remember you either. Do you think they are going to help you find a job?

Utilize your student orgs.

Throughout your involvement with student organizations, did you have the opportunity to attend any company visits? Were any presentations made by speakers from companies you would like to work for? Did you meet with them after their presentation, exchange contact information and keep at least a casual communication line open with them? This is where having that relationship can pay off when you approach them with your desire to find employment with their firm. They can be your inside advocate when a plum position opens up.

Make your part time work full time work.

If you work part time throughout college, and it is in any way within your field of interests, is there an opportunity to move to full time employment? For many, this is a great step to ensure that, after you've crossed the graduation stage and have your diploma, you have some form of employment that can help you earn an income, even if temporarily while you look for the more appropriate position for your career interests.

Intern your way in.

Internships are a fantastic way to get into a company. Under these programs, you work (sometimes even for free) within a company that you consider to be a potential employer, in a field that is aligned with your major. Very often you can flip an internship into a full time job and a great career, because the company has had a long period of time to see your work ethic, the quality of the work you do, and how well you fit in with the company culture. It saves them so much time and money knowing they are bringing a high-performing intern into the fold than risk bringing someone in from outside the firm that may or may not perform to their standards. Remember to make sure you target the companies and internship positions just like you would a regular, full time position. And take on the mindset that your internship is like an extended job interview. Because news alert: it is.

Recently it has become vogue to participate in a rotational development program. Under these programs, students rotate through a variety of departments, working with myriad people, teams and projects, and get a very thorough understanding of the business, its culture, its divisions and how they all interrelate – all within an intense, 1-2 year cycle. The companies running these programs often seek the best, the brightest, and those that are considered leaders among their peers (translation: not only get involved with student organizations, but preside over them as well). And while they might not pull you into the program until your final semester or after you graduate, it is not uncommon to turn an internship into a consideration for one of these programs. And consider that the employees who finish the rotational programs are often earmarked for faster promotions and greater opportunities, and they most definitely are among the protected groups when companies have to down-size or right-size.

Getting the right position to kick start your career means getting a very early head start. You are competing against fellow students and experienced workers, so it takes a lot of effort, a lot of elevator pitches, a lot of job applications and a lot of visits to Career Services and the people in your network to find that perfect start to a fabulous career. The sooner you start the better.

11   FOR PARENTS ONLY

One minute you're caressing your helpless little child in your arms, and the next, you're watching them graduate from high school, and not looking so helpless anymore. The time flew by. And now they're off to college and then on to adulthood, to have their own families, careers, successes and failure. And taxes. Don't forget taxes.

There are some things that you can do to set up your son or daughter for a better financial future and lower debt expenses after they graduate. The last thing you want is to see your child get that coveted Harvard business degree, only to get crushed by enormous student debt. The actions you take when your child is still in your care can make all the difference if they are getting on, or getting by.

Preparation starts at childbirth.

There are steps you can take when your child first arrives into this world that can make college finances easier when they head off to university in your old beater. Besides the subtle hints to your newborn of the great expectations you have for them, like the Stanford onesie or Oxford bib, you can take material steps in setting them up with a financial savings account to have some funds in their coffer when they (finally!) leave your nest.

In the US, 529 savings plans, so named after section 529 of an Internal Revenue Service code, allow for saving money in a tax-deferred account. That money is invested in underlying investments (typically mutual funds) which hopefully grow over the long term as those investments aggregate value. Think of it as analogous to a 401(k) for your child's education. When monies are distributed from that account for education-related expenses, they are tax-exempt. Those expenses include tuition and fees, and can also include books, equipment, supplies, and under specific rules, room and board. And while it is a US institution, some foreign universities accept this as well.

It should be noted that the money you place into this savings vehicle is not tax-deferred or tax-exempt from your income. You place post-tax funds into the 529 savings plan, which grow tax-deferred. If your designated beneficiary (your son, daughter, step-child, adopted child or whomever you designate the fund for) utilizes the funds for school, then no further taxes are paid.

Many states do allow you to include your contributions to a 529 plan as tax deductible, in full or a portion of the state tax liability. Get familiar with your state's tax laws, and if you file in a state that allows the deduction, take advantage. Federal income taxes do not release contributions from your tax liability. Damn the man.

As the 529 account is effectively owned by you, you do have the right to withdraw from that account, no questions asked. Just beware that, as it is not being used by your designated beneficiary for education purposes, then the earnings from that account are taxes as income tax and a 10% penalty is assessed. The system is set up to encourage you to save, discourage you from using it as a bank account, but at the same time making it available for financial emergencies.

In some states, the 529 plan includes a "prepaid" option, in which you can effectively purchase tuition to an in-state public university at today's cost, regardless of when your beneficiary will attend. Just beware that the credits only apply to in-state schools, though most participating states have a "transfer of value" option should the student choose to go to a college across state borders. Many caveats exist from state to state, and those rules change somewhat from time to time, so it is important to familiarize yourself with the rules applicable to your state.

While it is perhaps the most cost-efficient option, it makes several assumptions, such as education costs continuing to rise, your continued residency within your state, your beneficiary agreeing to attend a public university within your state of residence, and so on. A breakdown in any of these assumptions might mean forfeiting over some of your hard earned money. So consider your finances, your family, your own career path, and your options carefully before pulling the trigger on this.

Help select the career and school.

Your very gifted son may be born to be the best trial lawyer on earth, but if he doesn't get into the right schools, they may never reach their full potential. Frequent, honest conversations about your child's aspirations (even if they aspire to blast storm troopers forever) will help them make better decisions about their career, and thus, their education. For me, regular talks with my father about what kind of life I wanted to lead, what I wanted to do for fun and what I was good at helped me to articulate the outlines of a career when I was still in grade school. I propose that regular conversations about what your child wants to be, likes to do for fun, wants to own or do (their bucket list), and wants to be known for, will help them start thinking about their future in a way that will help them make the best decisions for their own future.

Many students find through these conversations that their love of poetry may not be able to afford the Maserati they dream of parking in their garage, so they might be better off with that pharmacy degree than a liberal arts degree. Likewise, the student who cares little of material wealth, but craves cultural exchange, might be best served getting that linguistic anthropology degree than forcing themselves through an unfulfilling legal degree. Defining those aspirations helps to narrow the vector of career paths, and that helps narrow the choice of schools. You can help them research and define the best schools for their degree, giving them a great opportunity for future success.

Please – do not push your child to do what you do. If they want to follow in your footsteps - fantastic. If they want to strike out on their own career path – support them.

Taxes. To file dependent or independent – that is the question.

If not already, your child will soon learn the old adage about death and taxes. Their first job wiping tables at the local diner, or valeting your buddies' Audis at the country club, will bring them to the unfortunate reality that taxes are inevitable. However, while our court system and tax code states that you cannot evade taxes, you can avoid them. One way is to define how your family and your student file taxes.

Throughout their childhood you have no doubt listed them in your tax filings as dependents. Each time a child was born, you at least celebrated the fact that, with another mouth to feed also came another consideration (translation: relief) when filing for your tax return. But as your child is getting ready to finish high school and pursue higher education, be aware that your treatment of them as a dependent on your tax return might remove them from candidacy for many needs-based scholarships and grants.

If your child were to, say, file independently on their taxes, and have a different residential address, then their applications for Pell grants and many scholarships would illustrate that their income is exactly what they made in the last calendar year, versus what they made plus what you made in the last calendar year. So under this theme, while you lose some tax relief on your own taxes, your student might be open to many grants and scholarships that would otherwise be unavailable to them. Talk with your accountant or tax advisor to see if this approach is right for you. For some, it is not, but for others, it might help defray the cost of education.

FAFSA is on you.

If you have been claiming your child as a dependent right up to their high school graduation day, then you will need to provide information on your child's FAFSA application. The Free Application for Federal Student Aid (FAFSA) is a federal form that your child can complete to gain access to be considered for certain grants and scholarships, not to mention federal student loans. It requires tax information, and if your child is a dependent, then it requires some of your tax information. Do not wait for your student to head off to State before completing this document. It should be done long before he or she graduates high school. For many scholarships – even private ones – a copy of the FAFSA is requested, or at least the information from it. And it should be completed and submitted each year, so that your information is updated. Consider it part of your tax filing activities.

Grants and scholarships are free money.

Help your student get into the mindset that grants and scholarships are free money, and that the efforts of filling out all those application forms are well worth the time and energy. For many students, this is their first experience at doing something of this nature, so a little guidance and encouragement from the parents is often needed. Show them the return on their effort when they get their first scholarship. Teach them to calculate their scholarship amount by the estimates hours of effort to arrive at an approximate tax-free dollars per hour. Compare that to what many high-paying jobs pay to illustrate the lucrative and valuable nature of applying for every scholarship they can. It is a numbers game – the more scholarships and grants your student applies for, the better their odds.

Consider your network of friends and business associates. Who do they know who might know someone who knows someone who is looking for a good scholarship candidate? Spread the word to everyone – get them looking for scholarship money on you and your student's behalf. Crowd source that education funding!

Nothing says I love you like a '98 Camry.

You may think your student needs a car for school. In some cases, it's not a bad idea. But automobiles are a big expense – one which the typical college student can ill-afford. Consider this: those wheels don't need to be shiny new, nor hold a set of Z-rated tires. While your heart may want to reward your high school graduate with a brand new Camaro, and your mind may want to rest easy that the new car will be trouble-free, your wallet and insurance provider may tell you that purchasing a new vehicle for your 18 year old might not be the best financial decision. Often times a used car can be found that is reliable, easy to repair and low on insurance premiums. If you can avoid a vehicle altogether - even better. That's money not spent on insurance, oil changes and car washes that might be put towards helping out with some of those college bills. Research the university and get a feel for its surroundings to determine this. If all the classes and plenty of jobs can be found within a bike ride's distance, then perhaps an investment into a sturdy Schwinn and an umbrella will be the best money spent on transportation. Look Ma! No parking fees!

Rent vs. buy.

For the financially astute, there is the housing question. Does my student live on campus? Off campus? In the dorms? On a couch? In a van in the parking lot? If you already have experience owning a rental property, and have the means, consider purchasing a home near the school as a real estate investment. Your student can live there free-of-charge (or he/she pays rent and you gift it back in the form of a scholarship), and any additional space can be leased to roommates. Know up front that college students may not be the kindest to property that they do not own, but with a little involvement (and a good list of plumbers, electricians and other home service providers on speed dial) you can help save your student some college expenses while simultaneously generating a little unearned income on the side. After your student graduates, you can sell the house or continue to manage it as a rental property. It's not for everyone, but for some, it is a keen way to minimize expenses, and possibly even pad the wallet in the process.

We have a diploma. What next?

Your little child goes off to college, studies hard, works a side job, gets involved, makes good grades, and before you know it, you're attending their graduation ceremony. What now?

They will very likely still need a little help from you. Unless they are blessed with a top-paying first job right out of college, they may struggle for a few months while they seek and obtain employment. Your helping hand during this time not only shows them how much you love them, but guides them down the right path to get their career off the ground. As with scholarships, leveraging your network can make a huge difference in the number and quality of opportunities for your son or daughter. Reach out to your network of friends and business acquaintances as your child is nearing graduation. Raise awareness of what your student is studying, and what they want to do. Make introductions. Grease palms. As the saying goes, it's not what you know – it's who you know. True, it is your child's future and not your own. They should own it. Just keep in mind that they will choose your nursing home!

The best of luck to you and your family in finding the right school, for the right price, and getting a great degree without the crushing burden of student loans creating a headwind while you get your career off the ground. With the simple, actionable steps outlined in this book, and some of your own creativity and ingenuity, you can make the most of your education. You can do it!

ABOUT THE AUTHOR

Lorenzo Ruccetti is a consultant and entrepreneur. He earned a Bachelors degree from a small, little-known university and Masters from a large, nationally-ranked university. His professional experience includes technology consulting & implementation, investment banking, fund management, strategic consulting and leadership development. His passions include driving classic automobiles, travel, great friends and great experiences. He lives in Houston with his family and bikes to work – even in the summer.

College on a Dime

College is a time for maximizing your education and future opportunities, not maximizing your student loans.

Too often today's graduates leave school with crushing student debts, limiting economic and social potential in ways never seen before in the US. But it does not have to be so bleak! College on a Dime shows you some of the simple, logical steps anyone can take to reduce or remove college debt from the college experience.

This second edition is updated to include the latest in tax considerations and tuition planning to ensure you have updated information at your disposal.

Finally, a practical guide to monitoring and controlling student debt. Roccetti has distilled down what matters most in choosing the right university and making the most of it.
- Christine M., mother of 3 college students

This book combines all the useful information you need into one easy to access location. Nothing in this book is novel, nor is it rocket science. It's better - it's useful.

- Bradley K., engineering student

Ruccetti makes accessible those techniques and practices that help to maximize the college experience without maximizing the debt load. I really appreciate the connection made between working, playing, and starting a career - nothing done in college is done without purpose.
- Justin R., MBA student

ISBN 9780998214207

90000 >

9 780998 214207